iDentities

PAUL SELIGSON, LUIZ OTÁVIO BARROS
and **ALASTAIR LANE**

STUDENT'S BOOK & WORKBOOK
COMBO EDITION

1A

Language Map – Student's Book

		Speaking / Topic	Grammar	Vocabulary / Strategies	Writing
1	1.1	What's the story behind your name?		Family: compound words and phrasal verbs	
	1.2	Do / Did you get along with your parents?	Using -ing forms: subjects, verbs, and expressions	Common uses of get	
	1.3	How many pets have you lived with?		Suffixes for nouns and adjectives	
	1.4	What difficult people do you know?	Using the infinitive with adjectives: active and passive sentences		
	1.5	Do you still make voice calls?		Developing an argument (1)	An effective paragraph: topic sentences; using connectors
2	2.1	What's most on your mind right now?		Noun modifiers: nouns and adjectives; expressing surprise	
	2.2	Do you worry about your diet?	Using noun, verb, and sentence complements	Expressions for food habits	
	2.3	Who's the smartest person you know?		Describing ability; reference words	
	2.4	Do you enjoy science fiction?	Degrees of certainty: *may, might, must, can,* and *could*		
	2.5	What was the last test you took?		Expressing advantages and disadvantages; agreeing and disagreeing	A for-and-against essay: listing pros and cons, contrasting, and reaching a conclusion
	Review 1 p.26				
3	3.1	Do you get embarrassed easily?	Narrative style	Physical actions; creating suspense	
	3.2	How often do you take selfies?	Past narration: simple, continuous, and perfect tenses; spoken grammar	Longer numbers	
	3.3	What invention can't you live without?		Words to describe inventions; binomials: repeated words, opposites, and related words	
	3.4	What was your favorite activity as a child?	Describing past habits and states: simple past, *used to,* and *would*		
	3.5	What makes you really happy?			Telling a story (1): linking words to sequence events
4	4.1	Are you ever deceived by ads?		False advertising: phrasal verbs; developing an argument (2)	
	4.2	Are teachers important in the digital age?	Conjunctions to compare and contrast ideas: *although, (even) though, despite, in spite of, unlike, while,* and *whereas*		
	4.3	What was the last rumor you heard?		Time expressions; similes	
	4.4	How would you describe yourself?	Reflexive pronouns with *-self / -selves;* reciprocal actions with *each other / one another*	Avoiding repetition	
	4.5	How many pairs of glasses do you own?		Figurative expressions	A product review: making generalizations
	Review 2 p.48				

Language Map – Student's Book

	Speaking / Topic	Grammar	Vocabulary / Strategies	Writing
5	5.1 What's your biggest life decision so far?		Collocations with verbs to discuss adversity; building a narrative	
	5.2 What would you love to be able to do?	Imaginary situations (1): *wish* and *if only*	Expressing encouragement	
	5.3 How important is a college degree?		Expressing negative ideas; prefixes: *over-*, *under-*, and *inter-*	
	5.4 Did you make any mistakes today?	Imaginary situations (2): mixed conditionals		
6	5.5 How lucky are you?			Telling a story (2): using a good range of adjectives
	6.1 Have you ever Googled yourself?		Verbs and expressions for online privacy	
	6.2 Do you worry about privacy?	Using passive structures: *be*, modal verbs, and *have*	Responding to an argument	
	6.3 What makes you suspicious?		More privacy words and expressions	
	6.4 Are you into social media?	Question words with *-ever*: *who*, *what*, *which*, *when*, and *where*		
	6.5 Who do you share your secrets with?			A *how to ...* guide: giving specific directions
Review 3 p.70				

Grammar expansion p.138

Selected audio scripts p.162

Workbook contents

Unit 1	Page 3
Unit 2	Page 8
Unit 3	Page 13
Unit 4	Page 18
Unit 5	Page 23
Unit 6	Page 28
Selected audio scripts	Page 63
Answer key	Page 67

Phrasal verb list p.119

1 » What's the story behind your name?

1 Listening

A Answer the title question. Do any of the photos remind you of your own family?

> My mother named me George after George Clooney. She's always been a fan. It means "farmer" in Greek.

Common mistake

> The second photo ~~remembers~~ *reminds* me of my family.

B ▶ 1.1 Listen to the start of a documentary about families. Choose the correct title.

☐ *All you need is love* – why family still matters in the U.S. today.
☐ *Everybody's changing* – a look at 21st-century American families.

C Read *Family members*. Do you have all of these relatives in your family?

Family members

You can use the bold words and prefixes to form different family words:
- I love my husband, but I find his mother really difficult. Is she a typical mother-**in-law**, I wonder.
- I grew up an **only** child, but Dad and his new wife had twins! Now I have not just one **half**-brother, but two! My **step**mother was as surprised as I was!
- I was raised by a **single** mom. My dad died before I was born.

D ▶ 1.2 Listen to the second part and order the photos 1–3. There's one extra family.

E ▶ 1.2 Listen again. T (true), F (false), or NI (no information)? Who do you think had the most difficult childhood?
1. Marco lived in a spacious apartment in Manhattan.
2. Marco and his stepfather have always been friendly with each other.
3. Karin's family used to make a lot of money.
4. Karin sometimes wishes she'd had a different adolescence.
5. Josh was very close to his grandma and his aunt.
6. Josh probably never met his great-grandmother.

> The one whose childhood sounded the most diffifult to me was …

♪ Hey brother, There's an endless road to rediscover. Hey sister, Know the water's sweet but blood is thicker

1.1

F Make it personal Do you agree with 1–4? Give examples.
1 "Family doesn't necessarily mean mother and father."
2 "Love is love. I know they say 'Blood is thicker than water,' but genetics makes no difference at all."
3 "Parents shouldn't prioritize their careers over their kids."
4 "In my experience, older parents have just as much energy as younger parents."

> I agree with the second one. Blood relationships are not the most important thing.

> Yeah, absolutely. I have an adopted sister and we adore each other.

2 Vocabulary: Family

A ▶ 1.3 Match the bold expressions in each group to their definitions. Listen to check.

1 Jeff and I didn't **get along** at all.
2 We always **made up** a few minutes later.

a ☐ become friends again after an argument
b ☐ have a good relationship

3 I **looked after** her while Mom and Dad were at work.
4 I think she really **looks up to** me.

c ☐ take care of somebody / something
d ☐ respect or admire

5 I was **brought up** by my grandmother.
6 I guess it **runs in the family**.

e ☐ care for a child and help him / her grow up
f ☐ be a common family characteristic

B In pairs, using only the photos and bold words, remember all you can about each family. What can you guess about the extra family?

> I think the boy is older than the girl.

C Complete questions 1–6 with the bold words in **A**, changing the verb tense and form as necessary.

What do your families have in common?
1 As a child, were you _brought up_ with lots of strict rules?
2 Today, who do you really _____ in your family? Why do you admire him / her?
3 Are there any family members you don't _____ with?
4 Have you ever had an argument with a relative? How long did it take you to _____ ?
5 Do / Did you ever have to _____ younger / aging relatives? Do / Did you enjoy it?
6 Can you think of one physical characteristic that _____ ?

D Make it personal Read *Phrasal verbs*. Then in pairs, ask and answer the questions in **C**. Ask follow-up questions, too. How many things in common?

Phrasal verbs

Remember phrasal verbs are either separable (**bring up** a child = **bring** a child **up**) or inseparable (**look back on** my childhood). Most two-particle phrasal verbs are inseparable:
I really **look up to** my father / him.
Try saying the sentence out loud. If it sounds wrong, the verb might be inseparable:
    look after my kids
Could you l~~ook my kids after~~ while I'm away?

> As a child, were you brought up with lots of strict rules?

> Well, my parents were really strict with me, but they let my little brother do anything he wanted.

1.2 Do / Did you get along with your parents?

3 Language in use

A Which uses of *get* below are you familiar with? Which sentences are true for you?

> **Common uses of *get***
> 1 *receive* or *have*: I never **got** an allowance.
> 2 *become*: I **get** bored during family meals.
> 3 *be able to*: When I was younger, I never **got** to drive Mom's car.
> 4 *arrive*: My parents insist I **get** home by 10 p.m.
> 5 *understand*: No one in my family **gets** me.

1 "I want you to feel I'm your friend, not just your mother."

2 "So ... when are we going to meet your girlfriend? I'm getting impatient!"

3 "I don't get it! I've been talking for hours, and all I get to hear from you is 'whatever'."

4 "Just because all your friends are doing it doesn't mean you should."

B When did you last hear / say the quotes in 1–4? Remember any similar ones?

> Here's one: "I'll take away your (phone) unless you do as you're told."

C ▶ 1.4 Read Carol's review and match quotes 1–4 in **B** with her son's advice a–d. Listen to check.

Carol's "in a nutshell" book reviews  HOME LOGIN

Desperate parents learn how to deal with their teenage kids

Basically, I'm doing it all wrong at home!

In a nutshell ... the practical value of *Teenagers Explained*

What I've learned

a ☐ It's no use pushing your teenagers to talk. Just do your own thing, maybe in the same room. They'll start a conversation with you when they feel like it.

b ☒ 1 Give up trying to be one of them. They expect you to be their role model, someone they can look up to. And, please, don't even try to be cool. You're not.

c ☐ In this case, pressuring teens will get you nowhere. You'll meet her when the time is right. End of story.

d ☐ Remember: Teens have trouble dealing with re**jec**tion. They're building their i**den**tities and want to belong and to feel accepted.

D Make it personal In pairs, answer 1–4. Do you generally agree with the advice in **C**?
1 What's your favorite piece of advice?
2 Would you like to read the book?
3 Who in your family "gets" / "got" you as a teen?
4 Summarize your family "in a nutshell."

> I really like "It's no use pushing your teenagers to talk." I think they need to pick the right time.

♪ Tonight, We are young. So let's set the world on fire. We can burn brighter than the sun

1.2

4 Grammar: Using -ing forms

A Read and match 1–4 to examples a–d in Carol's review.

Common mistake
I have a hard time ~~to deal~~ *dealing* with my son.

Using -ing forms: subjects, verbs, and expressions		
1 as subject of a sentence	c	**Raising teenagers** is a challenge. **Not listening to them** is the worst thing you can do.
2 after a phrasal verb		If she doesn't want to talk, **carry on doing** what you're doing.
3 in a negative point of view		**It's no good / It's not worth / There's no point arguing** with teenagers.
4 in some expressions of difficulty		Parents **have difficulty / a hard time talking** to children. **I can't help saying** yes, no matter how hard I try to say no.

» Grammar expansion p.138

B ▶1.5 Rephrase Carol's advice to her son 1–6 (before the book!) using an -ing verb as subject. Choose from these verbs, adding a preposition if necessary. Listen to check.

| do   eat   hang out   listen   read   risk (v)   spend |

"Eating fruit every morning is good for you."

1 "Fruit every morning is good for you."
2 "Too much time in front of that computer will hurt your eyes."
3 "Good literature will help you write better."
4 "Loud music can damage your ears."
5 "Too much exercise isn't good for you."
6 "Those guys will get you into trouble."

Hmm ... I hear this one almost every day.

C ▶1.6 Rewrite 1–5 using the expressions in bold. Listen to check. Do you think Carol became a better parent after the book?

1 Don't try to convince me. [**no use**] *It's no use trying to convince me.*
2 Continue to do what you were doing. [**carry on**]
3 It's hard not to wonder why you've been so quiet lately. [**can't help**]
4 Are you finding it hard to sleep? [**having trouble**]
5 It's not a good idea to live in the past. [**not worth**]

D Make it personal Choose a situation and role play a parent / teen conversation. Use expressions from the grammar box and C.

1 Teen: You want to go abroad on your own.

2 Parent: Your son / daughter never helps around the house.

3 Teen: You don't want your mom / dad to remarry.

4 Parent: The last phone bill was way too high.

Mom, there's something I've been meaning to tell you. You see, I ...

5 Teen: You want to drop out of school and get a job instead.

6 Parent: You don't like the people your son / daughter has been hanging out with.

... And that's my final answer. There's no point even mentioning it again!

1.3 How many pets have you lived with?

5 Reading

A In pairs, do you know people who have pets like this? Why do so many people treat their pets as equal members of the family?

My cousin has a birthday party for her dog every year. It's no use trying to stop her!

B ▶ 1.7 Read and complete the discussion forum with 1–4. Listen to check. In pairs, practice the pronunciation of the highlighted words.

1 owning a pet is good for your health
2 pets can help children develop emotionally
3 pets can teach us how to be responsible
4 owning a pet helps you meet new people

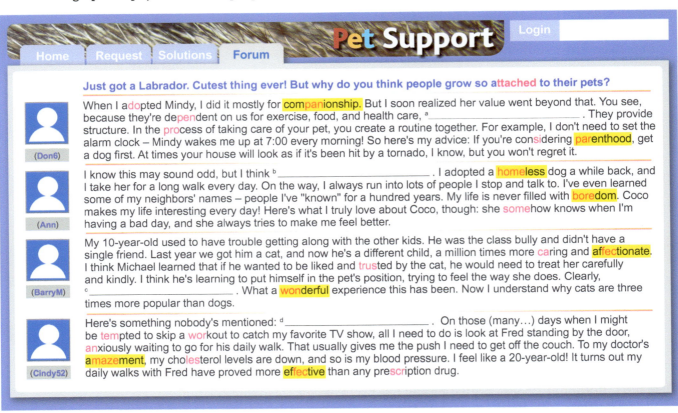

Pet Support   Login ____

Home | Request | Solutions | Forum

Just got a Labrador. Cutest thing ever! But why do you think people grow so attached to their pets?

(Don6) When I adopted Mindy, I did it mostly for companionship. But I soon realized her value went beyond that. You see, because they're dependent on us for exercise, food, and health care, ᵃ_____ . They provide structure. In the process of taking care of your pet, you create a routine together. For example, I don't need to set the alarm clock – Mindy wakes me up at 7:00 every morning! So here's my advice: If you're considering parenthood, get a dog first. At times your house will look as if it's been hit by a tornado, I know, but you won't regret it.

(Ann) I know this may sound odd, but I think ᵇ_____ . I adopted a homeless dog a while back, and I take her for a long walk every day. On the way, I always run into lots of people I stop and talk to. I've even learned some of my neighbors' names – people I've "known" for a hundred years. My life is never filled with boredom. Coco makes my life interesting every day! Here's what I truly love about Coco, though: she somehow knows when I'm having a bad day, and she always tries to make me feel better.

(BarryM) My 10-year-old used to have trouble getting along with the other kids. He was the class bully and didn't have a single friend. Last year we got him a cat, and now he's a different child, a million times more caring and affectionate. I think Michael learned that if he wanted to be liked and trusted by the cat, he would need to treat her carefully and kindly. I think he's learning to put himself in the pet's position, trying to feel the way she does. Clearly, ᶜ_____ . What a wonderful experience this has been. Now I understand why cats are three times more popular than dogs.

(Cindy52) Here's something nobody's mentioned: ᵈ_____ . On those (many…) days when I might be tempted to skip a workout to catch my favorite TV show, all I need to do is look at Fred standing by the door, anxiously waiting to go for his daily walk. That usually gives me the push I need to get off the couch. To my doctor's amazement, my cholesterol levels are down, and so is my blood pressure. I feel like a 20-year-old! It turns out my daily walks with Fred have proved more effective than any prescription drug.

C Re-read the discussion forum. Write the people's names.

1 __Ann__ is feeling more connected to her community.
2 _____ is not naturally inclined to an active lifestyle.
3 _____ thinks pets can prepare you to raise children.
4 _____ thinks having a pet can help you develop empathy.
5 _____ thinks pets are intuitive.

D Exaggeration is often used for emphasis. Find one example in each paragraph.

At times your house will look as if it's **been hit by a tornado.**

E Make it personal Do you know anyone who has experienced any of the four benefits of pet ownership in B? Can you think of any others?

Me! Number 4! I met my wife while I was buying tropical fish in a pet shop.

♪ It's been a hard day's night and I've been working like a dog

6 Vocabulary: Suffixes

A ▶ 1.8 Read *If you know suffixes*. Then scan **5B** and put the highlighted words in the chart according to their stress. Listen to check. How did you identify the part of speech?

> **If you know suffixes, you can …**
> 1. recognize parts of speech (noun, verb, adjective, etc.).
> 2. infer meaning (e.g., *less* = without / *careless* = without care).
> 3. expand your vocabulary by "anglicizing" similar words from other languages (Spanish *–miento* = English *–ment*: *movimiento* = *movement*).

Nouns
achieve**ment**
annoy**ance**
exist**ence**
fail**ure**
friend**ship**
happi**ness**
neighbor**hood**
secur**ity**
star**dom**

Adjectives
affection**ate**
care**less**
compar**ative**
courage**ous**
effect**ive**
help**ful**
prevent**able**

Nouns		Adjectives	
1 ☐ ☐ *boredom*	3 ☐ ☐ ☐ _____	5 ☐ ☐ *homeless*	7 ☐ ☐ ☐ _____
2 ☐ ☐ ☐ _____	4 ☐ ☐ ☐ _____	6 ☐ ☐ ☐ _____	8 ☐ ☐ ☐ _____

B ▶ 1.8 Listen again. Circle the correct rules.
1. Suffixes are [**always** / **never**] stressed.
2. Suffixes are [**often** / **rarely**] pronounced with a schwa /ə/.

C ▶ 1.9 Complete the text with words ending in the correct suffix. Listen to check. Do you agree with these research results?

> I'm a dog person, but I'm not very talkative.

Are you a **cat** person or a **dog** person?

A recent study found significant personality differ*ences*⁰ between those who self-identified as either dog people or cat people. Dog owners tend to be more extroverted, talk____¹, and approach____² than cat owners. They also have greater self-discipline and tend to score higher on assertive____³. Dog people like to stick to plans and are not particularly adventur____⁴.

Cat owner____⁵ is usually associated with open____⁶ to new ideas and different beliefs. Cat people are less predict____⁷, and more imagin____⁸, and they value their personal free____⁹ more than dog people. Because cats require less mainten____¹⁰ than dogs, cat people are more likely to be busy individuals who work a lot and have less time for close relation____¹¹.

D ▶ 1.10 **Make it personal** Listen to two friends playing a guessing game.
1. Who are they comparing? Check (✔) the correct answer after the beep.
   ☐ day people vs. night people ☐ couch potatoes vs. workout enthusiasts ☐ women vs. men
   ☐ motorcyclists vs. drivers ☐ small town people vs. big city people

2. In pairs, play the game:
   A Compare two groups. Include suffixes from **C**.
   B Guess who **A** is comparing.

> They tend to be really courageous, and they usually value their freedom.

> I think you're talking about …

1.4 What difficult people do you know?

7 Listening

A In pairs, what characteristics do difficult people have in common?

> Difficult people don't listen. They just talk.

B 🎧 ▶ 1.11 Listen to / Watch (0.00–2.46) Mary Bolster discuss difficult people and choose the correct answers.

1 Mary Bolster is …
- ☐ a psychologist.
- ☐ the editor of a health magazine.
- ☐ a doctor.

2 She talks about all of these difficult people except …
- ☐ salespeople.
- ☐ parents.
- ☐ bosses.
- ☐ coworkers.

Stacey Tisdale

Mary Bolster

C 🎧 ▶ 1.11 Listen / Watch again. True (T) or False (F)? Which of the speaker's reasons do you remember?

The best way to deal with difficult people is to …
1 try to change how you react to them.
2 just state the facts as neutrally as possible.
3 act hurt so they feel guilty.
4 make sure they know you're angry.

D Make it personal Have you ever followed the advice in the video? Did it work?

> Well, I once had a teacher who was very unreasonable, and I felt totally stressed out. I decided to …

8 Language in use

A ▶ 1.12 Read and complete the webpage with 1–4. Listen to check. Did you learn any new ways of dealing with difficult people?

1 It's important for you to put yourself in other people's positions
2 It's useful to give yourself time to think
3 These guidelines will make it easier for you to be understood
4 It feels good to be heard

THIS WEEK'S SURVIVAL TIPS	
Topic of the week	Dealing with difficult people
Coming up soon:	**Five easy ways to help you talk to difficult people:**
• Meeting your in-laws for the first time • New Year's Eve with the whole family • Your first day at school / work • Your first job interview • Passing your driver's test • An oral test in English • Saying "no" to people you love	a Pause and take a deep breath. Count to ten, if necessary. _____ and assess the situation. The less you react, the better. b Think like them. _____ so you can see the situation from another perspective. Listen carefully. If you were in their situation, what would it feel like? c Concede a little. Even if you agree with only one percent of what they are saying, let them know. Remember: _____ and have your opinion valued. d Watch your body language. Look the other person in the eye, smile if you can, and don't cross your arms. _____ . Remember: Successful communication is less than ten percent verbal. e Above all, be patient.

♪ I find it hard to tell you. I find it hard to take. When people run in circles, It's a very, very, Mad world, mad world

B Make it personal Which tip in A is best in your opinion? Can you suggest any others?

> I like the first one because I tend to lose my temper very easily – especially with my little brother.

9 Grammar: Using the infinitive with adjectives

A Read and check (✔) the correct rules in the grammar box.

Using the infinitive with adjectives: active and passive

	Active	Passive
adjective + (*not*) + infinitive	(a) It's **better to keep** calm.	(c) It's **hard not to be annoyed** by inconsiderate neighbors.
adjective + *for* + object + (*not*) + infinitive	(b) It's **easy for us not to listen** to people.	(d) It's **essential for people to be treated** with respect.

1 Use *be* + past participle in ☐ active ✔ passive sentences.
2 Use ☐ *not* ☐ *don't* to make negative sentences.
3 You ☐ *can* ☐ *can't* use the comparative form of adjectives.

Common mistakes

It's important for you ∧*to* show that you care.
It's advisable ~~don't~~ *not to* raise your voice.

▶ **Grammar expansion p.138**

B Re-read sentences 1–4 in **8A**. Which pattern in the grammar box (a–d) is each sentence?

It's important for you to put yourself in other people's positions – b

C ▶ 1.13 Read the end of the webpage in **8A** and correct four mistakes. Then listen to four students checking their answers in class.

> I hope these tips will make it easier ∧*for* you to handle some of the toxic people around you at home, school, or work. But keep in mind that it's important choose your battles wisely. There will be times when you will be successful and times when it will be very difficult for the other person to persuade. In those cases, it's no use trying. Remember: It's impossible you change someone. Change comes from within.

D Complete survival tips 1–6, making them negative or passive, if necessary.

How to survive your first job interview!
1 OK / you / be nervous *It's OK for you to be nervous.*
2 natural / they / be curious / you
3 important / arrive late
4 advisable / you / dress smartly
5 essential / keep checking / phone
6 important / intimidate / by the questions

E Make it personal Choose another situation from the website in **8A**. In groups, create five survival tips and add more details. Share them with the class. What's the most popular tip?

> If you're meeting your in-laws for the first time, it's important for you to arrive on time.

> It's no good … -ing

> … -ing isn't a good idea.

> It's advisable for you to …

> It's essential for you not to …

> There's no point in …-ing

1.5 Do you still make voice calls?

10 Listening

A ▶ 1.14 What do you think Steve Jobs' opinion on technology was? Listen to the beginning of a radio program to check.
- ☐ We should limit how much technology our kids use at home.
- ☐ We should encourage our kids to be as digitally connected as possible.

B ▶ 1.15 In pairs, list three possible arguments for Jobs' opinion. Listen to the rest of the interview. Were any of your ideas mentioned?

C ▶ 1.15 Listen again and fill in the missing words.

According to Dave Jackson, the guest on the radio program, ...

1. online __bullying__ is a real problem, but there are others.
2. too much texting can stop teens from developing _____.
3. texting can affect students' _____ progress.
4. electronic devices are making people _____.
5. it's _____ to chat every day by text with people you haven't met face to face.

Steve Jobs, co-founder, chairman and CEO of Apple Inc. (1955–2011)

D Which statement in **C** do you agree with most? In pairs, explain your choice. Any big differences?

> I believe online bullying is a terrible problem, but I agree, too much texting is, too.

11 Keep talking

A ▶ 1.16 **How to say it**
Complete sentences 1–4. Listen to check. Then repeat, sounding as convincing as you can.

Developing an argument (1)
1. For one __thing__, I believe digital technology is making people crueler.
2. What's _____, texting is making teens lazy.
3. Not to _____ the fact that we're unlearning how to communicate in the real world.
4. On _____ of that, our digital relationships are becoming too superficial.

B Read Dave Jackson's survey results and choose a statement you strongly agree with. List three arguments to support it.

Summary of results of survey on parenting skills

Statement	Agree	Disagree
It's important for children to receive a weekly allowance.	agree 53%	disagree 47%
Children should grow up as slowly as possible.	agree 82%	disagree 18%
It is also the parents' job – not only the school's – to educate children.	agree 37%	disagree 63%
It's no use choosing your children's careers for them.	agree 64%	disagree 36%
It's essential for parents to be strict with their children.	agree 51%	disagree 49%

C In groups, present your ideas using *How to say it* expressions. Your classmates will take notes on 1–3.
1. Were there any long pauses?
2. How many expressions were used?
3. Were there any important mistakes?

> It's important for children to get a weekly allowance to begin to appreciate money. For one thing ...

♪ Waiting for your call, Baby, night and day. I'm fed up, I'm tired of waiting on you.

1.5

12 Writing: An effective paragraph

A Read this paragraph from a student exam. Answer 1–3.
1. How many arguments does the writer use?
2. Which ones do you agree with?
3. Which words / expressions does the writer use to introduce each argument?

B Read *Write it right!* Then underline the topic sentence in **A**.

Write it right!

A topic sentence is the most important sentence in any paragraph because it summarizes the rest of the paragraph for the reader. The topic sentence is sometimes, but not always, the first sentence.

When building your argument, use connectors to add each new idea:

First,
To begin with,
↓
In addition,
Besides that,
Moreover, (more formal)
↓
Finally,
Lastly,

Name: ....

Date: ....

IT'S ESSENTIAL FOR SCHOOLS TO HAVE PHONE RULES

If you've ever had to look up a word online, need a quick calculator, or need to check the weather or a fact quickly, you know your phone can be a useful learning resource. However, I believe technology should be restricted in class for three reasons. First, playing games, posting Facebook® updates, and watching videos while the teacher and other students are talking is rude and disrespectful. If cell phones have to be turned off in movie theaters, libraries, during exams, at border controls, and on planes, why are classrooms any different? In addition, texting back and forth in class might generate unnecessary gossip and make everybody uncomfortable. People don't want to think they're being talked about behind their backs. Finally, it's important for students to get used to not going online whenever they want to. Self-discipline and the ability to focus are critically important in today's hyper-connected world. For all of these reasons, I strongly believe that schools should implement stricter phone rules.

C Read the *Common mistakes*. Then punctuate the beginning of the paragraph below.

Common mistakes

Hyper-connected kids get bored ~~easily,~~ *easily.*
~~in addition they~~ *In addition, they* find it hard to focus.

There are several advantages to texting over voice calls~~,~~ *. To* ~~to~~ begin with it allows shy people to say things they wouldn't otherwise besides that when you text someone you can think carefully about the message before hitting send.

D Your turn! Write a 100-word paragraph arguing in favor of the statement you chose in **11B**.

Before
Order your arguments clearly and logically. Write a topic sentence expressing the main idea of your paragraph.

While
Use a variety of connectors to link your ideas.

After
Proofread your paragraph carefully and check punctuation. Email it to a classmate before sending it to your teacher.

2 What's most on your mind right now?

1 Vocabulary: Noun modifiers

A ▶ 2.1 Listen and match people 1–6 to topics a–g. Pause and answer when you hear *Beep!* There is one extra topic.

Different people, different concerns

We asked people what was most on their minds.

a romantic relationships
b family dynamics
c material possessions
d financial problems
e physical appearance
f leisure activities
g peer pressure

 1 — b
 2
 3
 4
 5
 6

B ▶ 2.1 Listen again. In pairs, who do you relate to most?

> I felt sorry for the guy who had an argument with his father. I'm going through that, too.

C Read *Types of noun modifiers*. Then label the modifiers a–g from **A** as either A (adjective) or N (noun). Can you add three other combinations of these words?

Types of noun modifiers

We can use both nouns and adjectives to create new expressions:
a **family dinner** (noun + noun) = a dinner for the family
social issues (adjective + noun) = issues in society

> How about "family pressure"?

> That's a good one. There's a lot of pressure in my family!

romantic relationships – A

D **Make it personal** What's most on your mind these days? Share your thoughts in groups. Ask for and give more details. Any surprises?

> I can't stop thinking about my dog. She's been sick for a week now.

> Sorry to hear that. Have you taken her to a vet?

Common mistakes

I'm considering / thinking about ~~to go~~ *going* back to school.
Romantic ~~relations~~ *relationships* take up a lot of energy!
I'm thinking about ~~family's~~ / ~~families~~ *family* problems a lot.

- I'm considering …
- I keep worrying about …
- I think about … night and day.
- I can't seem to focus on anything but …

♪ All day long I think of things but nothing seems to satisfy. Think I'll lose my mind if I don't find something to pacify

2.1

2 Listening

A What's each person's problem in pictures 1–4? What do you think happened?

> This guy was driving with his feet out the window!

B ▶ 2.2 Listen to a conversation between April and her dad. Number the opinions 1–4 in the order you hear them.

☐ Young people listen to their friends more than adults.
☐ It's hard for young people to plan and organize so they can reach their goals.
☐ *1* Young people don't think about the consequences of their actions.
☐ Natural body rhythms in young people are different from adults.

C ▶ 2.2 Listen again. Who believes 1–6, Dad (D), April (A), or both (B)?
1 Young people's brains are immature until the age of 25.
2 April's last haircut was bad.
3 Teenagers are often tired during the day.
4 April is easily influenced by her friends.
5 Children under 25 should live with their parents.
6 Young people are adults at 18.

D Rephrase 1–6 using noun modifiers to replace the underlined text.
1 I'm worried about the work you're doing for school.
   I'm worried about your schoolwork.
2 I was just reading an article about the brain of the adolescent.
3 You can't argue with facts that are scientific.
4 They make decisions in an instant they often regret.
5 Our patterns of sleep, clocks regulating our bodies, are different.
6 Lots of crashes involving cars are caused by young drivers.

E In pairs, how many noun modifiers can you use to describe the pictures in **A**? Which reasons in **B** explain the situations? Similar opinions?

> She sure has an awful haircut! She clearly didn't think about …

F **Make it personal** Discuss young people's responsibilities.

1 ▶ 2.3 **How to say it** Complete these expressions from the conversation in **B**. Then listen to check.

Expressing surprise	
What they said	What they meant
1 I had no idea at ___all___ (that) …	I had absolutely no idea (that) …
2 It never _____ to me (that) …	I never thought (that) …
3 You've got to be _____ !	This is a joke, right?
4 It _____ me (that) …	It really surprises me (that) …

2 In groups, decide at what age young people should be able to do these things and why. Use *How to say it* expressions.

babysit   drive a car   get a tattoo   get married   join the army   travel abroad alone   vote

> It amazes me that some people say you should be 25 or over to drive a car. I'm 19 and I'm a really careful driver.

> Well, maybe you're the exception and not the rule.

2.2 Do you worry about your diet?

3 Language in use

A ▶ 2.4 Listen and fill in the missing words. As you listen, notice the silent /t/ at the end of some words.

the best thing   the biggest problem   the hardest thing

Sign in   Join

Online Quick Survey

Do you have a sweet tooth?

We asked our readers what sweet **treats** they can't resist. Here's what they told us!

I usually have an ¹_____ every afternoon. The best thing about it is that it wakes me up for my afternoon classes.
Carmen, 17

²_____ !! The biggest problem is **weight gain** if I have one every day.
Greg, 24

I love a big ³_____ for dessert in restaurants. The hardest thing is sharing it with other people!
Marcella, 16

I have two or three ⁴_____ a day. The good thing is the ⁵_____, which gives me energy. It **keeps me going**, and I really need it because I play a lot of sports.
Dieter, 19

⁶_____ is my favorite! Going to our local ⁷_____ is a **big deal** for my family. The best part is all the different ⁸_____, so it never gets boring!
Nancy, 18

There's definitely an advantage to ⁹_____ ! I eat a lot of them to pick me up. However, the **disadvantage** is that they make you feel even more tired later, when the effect **has worn off**.
Ben, 20

In my family, we don't have ¹⁰_____ like ice cream and cookies, only fruit. My mom says fruit has ¹¹_____ .
Jackie, 21

B Complete the definitions with the **highlighted** words from A. Change the form if neccesary.

1. To _keep_ someone _going_ (v) means to give someone strength to continue.
2. A _____ (n) is the opposite of an advantage.
3. It's a _____ (n) means it's important.
4. A _____ (n) is something that gives pleasure or enjoyment.
5. To _____ (v) means to diminish in effect.
6. _____ (n) is the process of becoming heavier.

C Make it personal Who in the survey do you identify with most / least? What foods can't you resist? Survey the class to find your top five.

> Do you have a sweet tooth?

> Not really, but I really can't resist pizza! It's such a great comfort food.

♪ I can eat my dinner in a fancy restaurant. But nothing, I said nothing can take away these blues

2.2

4 Grammar: Using noun, verb, and sentence complements

A Study the sentences 1–3 in the grammar box. Find five similar ones in the survey, and write N (noun), V (verb) or S (sentence) next to each. Then check (✔) the correct rules.

> **Noun, verb, and sentence complements to describe advantages and disadvantages**
>
> 1 The problem with cafés **is noise**. (N)
> 2 The good thing about going to one **is being able to sit down**. (V)
> 3 The best thing **is (that) they serve nice food**. (S)
>
> After *is*, the form of the verb is an ☐ **infinitive** ☐ **ing form**.
> When a sentence follows *is*, the word *that* ☐ **is** ☐ **isn't** optional.
>
> Be careful with subject-verb agreement, and make sure sentences have a subject!
> **One** of the best things about restaurants **is** good food.
> One disadvantage of **restaurants** is that **they are** often crowded.
>
> **Common mistakes**
> The best thing about ~~fruits~~ *fruit* (NC) is that ~~they have less~~ *it has fewer* calories (C) than chocolate.
>
> Remember that count (C) and non-count (NC) nouns are different!

» Grammar expansion p.140

B Match the sentence halves. Do you agree with the statements?

1 The best thing about energy drinks is …
2 The problem with fruit is …
3 The biggest advantage of vegetables is …
4 The most difficult thing about eating well is …
5 The worst thing about junk food is …

a ☐ that it's expensive, especially if it's organic.
b ☐ knowing what's good for you and what isn't.
c ☐ that they help you stay alert.
d ☐ that it's irresistible!
e ☐ vitamins and minerals, but less sugar.

> I definitely agree with the first one. And another good thing about them is …

C Complete 1–4 with your ideas. In groups, whose were the most original?

1 The best thing about paying taxes is … , but the worst thing is …
2 The most difficult thing about studying English is … , but the most rewarding thing is …
3 The easiest part of meeting someone new is … , but the hardest part is …
4 The biggest advantage of my neighborhood is … , but the biggest disadvantage is …

> The best thing about paying taxes is that it feels good to be honest, but …

D Make it personal Choices and more choices!

1 Note down the pluses and minuses of each choice (a–d). Then make a decision.

a On your birthday, would you rather go out to eat or throw a party at home?
b If you want to see a movie with your family, would you rather go to a theater or watch it on TV?
c If you want a new phone, would you rather buy it unlocked or sign up for a plan?
d On vacation, would you rather lie on the beach, hike in the mountains, or go sightseeing in your city?

2 Find a partner who thinks the opposite. Share your arguments. Use expressions from **A** and **B**. Can you change people's minds?

> Well, the good thing about having a party is that you can invite more people.

> Yes, but it's a lot of work.

3 Finally, take a class vote. Which choices win?

2.3 Who's the smartest person you know?

5 Vocabulary: Describing ability

A ▶ 2.5 Listen to a lecture on six types of intelligence. Number the pictures 1–6.

B ▶ 2.5 Guess the missing words in the notes (1–6) on the right. Be careful with verb forms. Listen again to check.

C Write the highlighted expressions from the notes in B in the chart. Then test your memory in pairs:

A Use the pictures and chart to describe the six types of intelligence.
B Prompt **A** and offer help when needed. Then switch roles.

		☺	☹
at	1	be good at	be bad / hopeless at (music / singing)
	2	_____	
	3	_____	
for	4	_____	have no talent for (sports / playing …)
of	5	_____	be incapable of (learning …)
to	6	_____	be unable to (learn …)

> Someone who has logical-mathematical intelligence is really good at …

Common mistake

I find it easy to speak / I'm good at speaking
~~I have facility to speak / speaking~~ in public.

NOTES

Intelligence types / people's abilities:

1 Lo**g**ical-mathe**mat**ical: They're good at analyzing and ___solving___ problems.

2 **Ver**bal-lin**guis**tic: They find it easy to tell stories and _____ new concepts.

3 **Mus**ical: They're capable of remembering whole songs and _____ notes and tones.

4 Bodily-kines**thet**ic: They often have a gift for drawing and _____ .

5 **Spa**tial: They're adept at interpreting graphs and _____ maps.

6 Inter**per**sonal: They're skilled at inter**act**ing with other people and _____ their emotions and intentions.

D Make it personal In pairs, answer 1–3.
1 Which are your two strongest types of intelligence? How do you know?
2 Which one(s) do you think you should work on? Have you tried?
3 Do you think it makes sense to divide intelligence into different types? Why (not)?

> I think my spatial intelligence is good. I find it easy to give directions, and I never get lost.

> I'm just the opposite. I can barely understand my GPS!

6 Reading

A ▶ 2.6 Read the introduction. Guess the author's answer to the question there. Then listen to or read the article to check.

FISH AND TREES: GARDNER'S MULTIPLE INTELLIGENCES REVISITED

Howard Gardner's theory of multiple intelligences was published in 1983. It is still relevant today and accepted by many as true. But is it a valid way of looking at learning?

Of all the memes I see on my Facebook® wall day after day, there's one that looks particularly clever. It claims that "Everybody's a genius, but if you judge a fish by its ability to climb a tree, you will think it's stupid." In other words, we're all gifted at different things, so we should concentrate on our strengths, not on our weaknesses. People with a high degree of musical intelligence, for example, will excel at playing instruments, but may be hopeless at expressing themselves in writing, or doing math problems in their heads. Fair enough. Who can argue against the notion that each and every one of us is different?

Maybe this explains why Gardner's theory is still popular. In a way, we all like to think of ourselves as unappreciated geniuses whose brilliance remains undiscovered. We're fish, and our teachers and bosses are making us climb trees. But are we really that special? Stephen Hawking is a genius. Mozart was a genius. The fact that my three-year-old can draw a four-legged horse on a rooftop doesn't make her a genius. It simply means she's skilled at drawing pictures of animals, which may or may not help her make a decent living in the future.

Worse still, the theory seems to reinforce the idea that some people have no talent for certain things and that little can be done about it. This, to me, denies the whole point of education, which is to enable people to master new skills and deal with challenges. In my view, you don't need highly developed linguistic intelligence to be able to write a clear essay, or a good degree of bodily intelligence to become a dancer or an athlete.

Any theory that overlooks the importance of motivation, passion, and hard work should not be taken seriously, I believe.

B Re-read. Infer which statements the author would agree with and write Y (yes) or N (no). Underline the evidence in the article.
1. We should only focus on what we're naturally good at.
2. People tend to underestimate their own intelligence.
3. Parents tend to overestimate children's talents.
4. Children with special talents generally become rich later in life.
5. Schools should focus on what students can already do well.
6. You can learn most things if you put your mind to it.

C Read *Reference words*. Then explain what the eight highlighted words in the text refer to.

> **Reference words**
>
> Reference words often refer back to a specific, stated word, but they can refer to a concept, too.
> You can't judge a **fish** by **its** ability to climb a tree. **This** idea makes perfect sense to me.
> (*Its* = the fish's ability; *This* = the fact that we can't judge a fish.)

D Make it personal Answer 1–3 in groups. Any surprises?
1. Choose a statement in **B** you agree / disagree with. Explain why.
2. How does / did your school deal with students' different abilities and learning styles?
3. Which skills do these jobs require? Which is the most important intelligence type for each?

actor   athlete   chef   manager   nurse   parent   politician   taxi driver   teacher

> I think it's really important for a teacher to be good at explaining things.

> I don't know. A teacher needs to be intuitive – you know, have a gift for reading people's expressions.

2.4 Do you enjoy science fiction?

7 Listening

A ▶ 2.7 Listen to three friends discussing a news report. Who's most convinced that intelligent alien life exists, Theo or Ruby?

B ▶ 2.7 Listen again and check (✔) the name(s). In pairs, share your opinion on these statements.

Who believes ...	Theo	Judd	Ruby
1 most UFO stories have a lot in common?		✔	✔
2 it's likely that there's some extraterrestrial life?			
3 maybe aliens talk to each other mentally?			
4 the pyramids were built by aliens?			
5 there's a lot of reliable evidence that aliens do exist?			
6 it's likely that if aliens exist, they are physically similar to us?			

C ▶ 2.8 Read the excerpts in the speech bubbles and guess Theo's story. Then listen and number the speech balloons (1–6). How close were you to guessing Theo's story?

[1] So I thought, "There must be someone following me."

[ ] Oh, come on! It can't have been a vacuum cleaner.

[ ] Walking the dog after midnight? You can't be serious!

[ ] You're saying it might have been a joke?

[ ] The whole thing must have been planned.

[ ] A toy? Yeah, that could explain the whole thing.

Let's see. It was late at night, and he thought somebody was following him. So he was walking outside, right?

Yeah, but what about the vacuum cleaner? What does it have to do with the rest of the story?

♪ Well, I dreamed I saw the silver spaceships flying in the yellow haze of the sun

2.4

8 Grammar: Degrees of certainty with modal verbs

A Study the grammar box and check (✔) the correct rules. Then identify the passive sentence in 7C.

> **Degrees of certainty:** *may, might, must, can,* and *could*
>
> | | Present | Past |
> |---|---|---|
> | **Maybe** it's true. | They **might / may (not) look** like us. | It **might / may (not) have disappeared**. |
> | **I'm pretty sure** it's true. | It **must (not) be** a UFO. | You **must (not) have felt** scared. |
> | I **really doubt** it's true. | You **can't / couldn't be** serious! | It **can't / couldn't have been** a UFO. |
>
> 1 Use a modal verb + *be / have been* + past participle to form ☐ active ☐ passive sentences:
>   Other planets **might be inhabited** by humans.   The scene **could have been captured** on video.
> 2 *Could* means *may* or *might* in the ☐ affirmative ☐ negative only:
>   It **could have been** a UFO. The scene **could have been captured** on video.

> **More about *can* and *could***
>
> *Can* is <u>not</u> used in the affirmative to express possibility:
> It **could / may / might be** an alien.

>> Grammar expansion p.140

B Rephrase 1–6 beginning with the underlined words.
1 I doubt <u>we</u> are alone in the universe.
  We can't (couldn't) be alone in the universe.
2 Maybe <u>there</u> is life on other planets.
3 Maybe <u>they</u> use a different form of communication.
4 I doubt <u>the pyramids</u> were built by aliens.
5 (If there are aliens out there), I'm pretty sure <u>they</u> look a lot like us.
6 I'm pretty sure <u>we</u> have been visited by extraterrestrials.

C Make it personal In pairs, rephrase the sentences you disagree with, using a different modal. Are you more like Theo, Ruby, or Judd?

> First one ... I think we might be alone in the universe. I mean, who knows.

> **Common mistakes**
>
> *been invented*
> That legend must have ~~invented~~ by our ancestors.
> *have*
> I think The Loch Ness Monster might ~~had~~ actually existed.

9 Pronunciation: Modal verbs in informal speech

A ▶ 2.9 Read and listen to the rules. Then listen to and repeat examples 1–3.

> In rapid, informal conversation, it's important to understand these common reductions:
> must have = *musta*   might have = *mighta*   could have = *coulda*
> In less informal speech, say *must've, might've,* and *could've*.

1 He <u>must have</u> been confused.   2 It <u>might have</u> been a joke.   3 It <u>could have</u> been a UFO.

B Make it personal Think of something hard to explain that happened to you or someone else. Share your stories in groups. Whose explanation is the most logical?

> And then when I opened the door, there was nobody there.

> Wow! That must have been scary. Were you alone at home?

2.5 What was the last test you took?

10 Listening

A ▶ 2.10 Answer 1–4 in the IQ quiz as fast as you can. Listen to two friends to check. For you, which was the hardest question?

IQ QUIZ
1 Which number should come next in this series: 25, 24, 22, 19, 15 …?
2 *Library* is to *book* as *book* is to …
   A copy   B page   C cover   D bookshop
3 Mary, who is 16 years old, is four times as old as her brother. How old will Mary be when she is twice as old as her brother?
4 Which of the following diagrams doesn't belong?

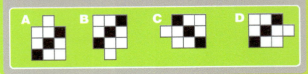

B ▶ 2.11 Listen to the rest of their conversation. Circle a or b.

1 Carol thinks IQ tests …
   a are boring.
   b have more disadvantages than advantages.

2 Flavio …
   a doesn't have strong feelings for or against IQ tests.
   b sees many advantages to IQ tests.

C ▶ 2.11 Listen again and complete 1–6 with one to three words.

Advantages	Disadvantages
1 Internet IQ tests are *fun*.	4 They focus on specifics like _____.
2 They _____ your brain.	5 They pay no attention to your _____.
3 They can help teens _____.	6 They might negatively affect your _____.

D 🌐 Go online and take an IQ quiz in English and check your score. Is there an argument in C you strongly (dis)agree with?

Common mistakes

took   got   stands for
I ~~made~~ one of those online tests and ~~took~~ a perfect score. IQ ~~signifies~~ Intelligence Quotient.

11 Keep talking

A Choose a question 1–6. Note down two advantages, two disadvantages, and your conclusion.
What are the advantages and disadvantages of …
   1 being considered the family genius?
   2 getting into college when you're very young?
   3 being rich and famous?
   4 being extremely good-looking?
   5 being very tall?
   6 being an only child?

B How to say it Share your views in groups using the expressions in the chart. Who has the best arguments?

Advantages	Disadvantages	Agreeing / Disagreeing
One of the best things about … is (that) …	The trouble with … is (that) …	Absolutely!
Another plus is (that) …	Another problem with … is (that) …	That's one way to look at it.
		I wouldn't be so sure.

> I think being an only child has more advantages than disadvantages. For one thing you get a lot of attention.

> Well, I wouldn't be so sure. The trouble with being an only child is you're lonely.

♪ I'm a science genius girl. I won the science fair. I wear a white lab coat. DNA strands in my hair

2.5

12 Writing: A for-and-against essay

A Read this upper-intermediate student's essay. Ignoring the blanks, find two arguments for tests and two against them.

1   Most schools in my country still evaluate students using formal tests. However, more and more schools are beginning to evaluate students based on their performance, instead. This includes essays, projects, presentations, and real-world activities. Some people think tests are a necessary evil, _while (whereas)_ others say students need to be evaluated after every class. Personally, I agree with the second group.

2   _____ tests is that they're objective and easy to grade, which is useful for teachers who teach large classes. _____ is that students with low scores can be given enough extra help before it's too late.

3   _____ , I believe _____ using test scores to evaluate students. First, students who do well might think they're better than everybody else, _____ students with lower grades might lose confidence and have a poor self-image. _____ tests is that they emphasize memorization, instead of creativity and social skills. When performance is evaluated continuously, every class is important. Students try harder, and teachers take more interest in every individual.

4   _____ , I believe formal tests should be replaced by continuous evaluation. This way, students can also evaluate themselves, and this is really the whole point of education.

B Read *Write it right!* Then complete the essay with items 1–8, changing the punctuation as necessary.

Write it right!

In a for-and-against essay, use expressions like these to help readers follow your train of thought.

Listing pros and cons	1 One advantage of … 2 A further advantage … 3 There are a number of drawbacks to … 4 Another disadvantage of …
Contrasting	5 On the other hand … 6 While … / 7 Whereas …
Reaching a conclusion	8 To sum up …

C Complete the guide with the numbers of the paragraphs 1–4.

- Present both sides of the question in paragraphs ___ and ___ .
- Give your own opinion in paragraph ___ and summarize it in paragraph ___ .

Common mistake

Some people are in favor of school ~~uniforms, on the other hand,~~ *uniforms. On the other hand,* ~~the other hand~~ others want to ban them.

D Complete 1–3 with an opinion of your own. Then compare sentences in groups. Any similarities?

1 While it's true that schools … , personally, I believe that …

2 Retiring early gives you a chance to reinvent yourself, whereas …

3 Living in a big city has both pros and cons. On the one hand, … On the other hand, …

E Your turn! Write a four-paragraph essay (250 words) discussing one of the questions in 11A.

Before
List the pros and cons. Order them logically. Anything you can add?

While
Write four paragraphs following the model in A. Use at least five expressions from B.

After
Post your essay online and read your classmates' work. What was the most popular topic? Similar arguments and conclusions?

Review 1
Units 1–2

1 Listening

▶ **R1.1** Listen to Joe and Amy and choose the best inferences A–D. What did they say that supports your answers? Check in **AS** R1.1 on p.162.

1 When he was a teenager, Joe probably did something ...
   A embarrassing but not serious.
   B dangerous and illegal.
   C motivating and exciting.
   D cool and fun.
2 Joe uses the expression "Need I say more?" because ...
   A he doesn't want to go into details.
   B he's already told the whole story.
   C he might have forgotten what happened.
   D he'd like to continue with his story.
3 Amy keeps the conversation going by ...
   A talking about herself.
   B showing interest.
   C being overly curious.
   D changing the subject.
4 Joe and Amy are probably ...
   A close friends.
   B brother and sister.
   C just getting to know each other.
   D teacher and student.

2 Grammar

A In pairs, rewrite 1–6 about Joe. Begin with the underlined words and use modal verbs.

1 Maybe <u>Joe</u> was arrested when he was 16.
2 I doubt <u>he</u> has a criminal record. He seems like such a nice guy.
3 I'm pretty sure <u>they</u> moved because of something more minor.
4 Maybe <u>his grandparents</u> liked change in general.
5 I'm pretty sure <u>his grandparents</u> had an interesting life.
6 I doubt <u>they</u> made much money, though.

B Role play the conversation between Joe and Amy, changing the details to those of a story you've heard or read about. Act out your conversation for the class. Whose is the most creative?

C Make it personal Write sentences with your opinion. Share in groups. Any disagreements?

1 The best thing about moving to a new city is ...
2 A problem with our school is ...
3 One advantage of this city (town) is ...
4 The most difficult thing about getting up in the morning is ...
5 A disadvantage of having a part-time job is ...
6 A good thing about having older parents is ...

3 Reading

Read the title. What do you think the article is about? Skim the article quickly. Were you right?

Science fiction may soon be fact!

Do great new developments in science start as science fiction? And does the creative process of science fiction encourage breakthroughs in science? According to the Center for Science and the Imagination (CSI) at Arizona State University, founded in 2012 to foster cooperation between writers, artists, and scientists, the answer to both questions may be yes.

Science fiction authors have a long history of imagining life-changing technology. Rockets for space travel were popular in science fiction long before they became reality, culminating in the Apollo mission that put a man on the moon in 1969. During the most exciting periods of innovation, science has had many "dreamers."

While space travel is still too expensive, other elements of science fiction stories have become part of everyday life. The "picture phone" of the 1964 World's Fair was a failure initially. For one thing, service was only available in three cities, and customers had to schedule screen time in advance. Calls were prohibitively expensive, with a three-minute call between New York and Washington, D.C. costing $16, or the equivalent of $120 today. By 1968, the project had been judged a failure. Yet today, free video calls over WiFi are a fact of life around the world.

Of course, much scientific innovation happens without science fiction stories. Future computers may be a big theme in science fiction today, but the foundations of modern computing were established in the 1940s and 50s. The most imaginative ideas may lack funding, and surprising innovation may happen spontaneously. Nevertheless, according to CSI, even though failed ideas can be expensive, scientists should be encouraged to keep dreaming.

4 Writing

Using the ideas in the article and three of the words or expressions below, write a paragraph to support the following statement.

Ideas that sound like science fiction today may be real tomorrow, and companies should fund scientists' innovative ideas.

| First, To begin with, | → | In addition, Besides, Moreover, | → | Finally, Lastly, |

5 Point of view

Choose a topic. Then support your opinion in 100–150 words and record your answer. Ask a partner for feedback. How can you be more convincing?

a You see many advantages to owning a pet. OR
   You think pets are a lot of unnecessary work.

b You feel there are far too many rude people using technology inappropriately. OR
   You feel technology is a wonderful modern invention.

c You think there's no such thing as types of intelligence, and you can learn anything if you put your mind to it. OR
   You think people have unique talents and should spend their time developing those.

d You don't believe what appears in science fiction will ever be real. OR
   You think the world is a mysterious place, and it's impossible to know what's true.

3

Do you get embarrassed easily?

1 Vocabulary: Physical actions

A ▶ 3.1 Read and match the highlighted verbs in the radio station's countdown to pictures a–g. Listen to check.

7 You get into the wrong classroom and sit there for a long time before realizing you're not supposed to be there. Then you leave in the middle of the lesson while all the students **stare** [b] at you. (Hugo, New Mexico)

6 You **push** [ ] doors that you should **pull** [ ] and vice versa, especially in a crowded room – twice, three, four times. I have a 50 / 50 chance, but, guess what, I always get it wrong. (Ana, Medellín)

5 You're in the middle of a boring lesson, and you're dying to break for coffee, so you **yawn** [ ] and **glance** [ ] at your watch – as discreetly as possible. Trouble is, the teacher sees you. And again. And again. (Bruce, London)

4 You think a spider has landed on you, so you **scream** [ ] at the top of your lungs – in a public place. And, of course, the spider is just a fly. (Amanda, São Paulo)

3 You're talking to a friend and **whisper** [ ] something to her so nobody can hear you – especially gossip! To your horror, she repeats what you said out loud, for the whole room to hear. (Gloria, Dallas)

2 You meet someone you don't know well, and neither one of you knows whether you should **hug** [ ], shake hands, or kiss – one, two, three, or (if you're French) even four times. So you go for the hug, and the other person extends his or her arm, or tries to kiss you. (Albert, Montreal)

1 You're running on the treadmill when suddenly you **trip** [ ] on your shoelaces and fall. Trust me, it's painful on your body and on your ego. (Tomiko, New York)

B Are the highlighted verbs a) movement, b) speech, or c) vision? Notice the preposition, if any, that goes with each verb. *stare (at) – vision*

> **Common mistake**
> Everybody looked / glanced / stared ~~to~~ *at* me when I fell.

C Do you agree with the station's ranking? Which stories would be in your personal top three?

> Not knowing how to greet people should be Number 1.

D **Make it personal** Embarrassing moments! In groups, use the pictures to ask and answer questions. Any surprises?

> Don't you hate it when you trip on your shoelaces, fall, and the whole room stares at you?

> Oh, yeah, that keeps happening to me. Once I fell down an airport escalator!

♪ And every glance is killing me. Time to make one last appeal for the life I lead. Stop and stare. I think I'm moving but I go nowhere

3.1

2 Listening

A ▶3.2 Listen to three friends doing activity **1C**. Which two stories from **1A** are they talking about?

B ▶3.3 Listen to the rest of the story. Answer 1–3.
1 Where did Marco go and why?   2 Who did he see here?   3 What did he do?

C ▶3.3 Listen again. What can you infer about Marco? Check (✔) the wrong statement.
☐ He sometimes goes to the movies alone.   ☐ He and his sister-in-law get along.
☐ He'd been looking forward to that movie.   ☐ Marco is a friendly person.

D ▶3.4 In pairs, how do you think the story will end? Listen to check. How close were you?

E Read *Narrative style*. Then underline seven examples in **AS** 3.3 and 3.4 on p.162.

> **Narrative style**
>
> When telling stories or jokes, we sometimes use present tenses to create a dramatic narrative effect. Don't mix present and past tenses in the same sentence.
>
>   *realize*   *'ve*
> Then I click "send" and ~~realized~~ I ~~had~~ sent a message to the wrong person, so I start to sweat.

F **Make it personal** Tell your own "embarrassing moment" story.

1 ▶3.5 **How to say it** Complete these expressions from Marco's story. Then listen, check, and repeat, first at normal speed and then faster. Be sure to use appropriate gestures.

Creating suspense			
After that		What next?	
1 The _____ thing I know (the woman moves three rows back.)		4 OK, go _____ .	
2 You _____ believe what happens next.		5 And _____ what?	
3 Before I _____ it, (everybody's staring at us).		6 So what _____ next?	

2 Choose an idea below for inspiration, or think of your own.

> You're never going to believe what happened to me! Last week …

   a Note down what happened, using the past tense.
   b In groups, tell your story. Use the present tense for dramatic moments.
   c Use physical action verbs and *How to say it* expressions.
   d Write each student's name on the "embarrassment continuum" and compare your rankings!

being caught doing something wrong   breaking something   texting / emailing the wrong person
forgetting your wallet   mistaking people   spilling drinks / food   forgetting appointments

EMBARRASSMENT CONTINUUM

Slightly awkward   I started to turn red.   Extremely embarrassing

>> 3.2 How often do you take selfies?

3 Language in use

A ▶ 3.6 Guess how these photos are connected. Listen to a radio show to check. How close were you?

Ellen DeGeneres   Bradley Cooper   Meryl Streep

> Hmm … Ellen's not a movie star, right? What's she doing there?

> Yeah. And I don't think Bradley Cooper has won an Oscar.

Longer numbers

In informal writing, longer numbers are sometimes simplified:
23**k** followers = 23 **thousand**
1.1**m** retweets = 1.1 **million**
2m **plus** views = **over** 2 million

B ▶ 3.7 Read *Longer numbers* and listen to the rest of the story. Which two longer numbers do you hear?

C In each paragraph, check (✔) the action that happened first. Did you hear the correct numbers?

DeGeneres then **posted** ☐ the photo online, and it reached nearly 800k retweets in about half an hour, temporarily crashing Twitter®. Before the three-and-a-half hour show **was** ☐ over, it **had become** ☐ the world's most retweeted photo ever, with 2m plus tweets. The selfie had just made history. "We're all winners tonight," said DeGeneres.

Was it 100% spontaneous? No one knows for sure. The photo was taken with a popular phone, so some people say it **was** ☐ a multi-million dollar deal with the phone company, which **had been sponsoring** ☐ the Oscars for years. Others believe it was totally unplanned.

HOW ABOUT YOU? WHAT DO YOU THINK?   LEAVE A MESSAGE ON OUR WEBSITE.

D Make it personal In pairs, answer 1–6. Any major differences?
1. Is the word *selfie* used in your language?
2. Should selfie sticks be banned?
3. Are you both into taking selfies? Looking at others' selfies?
4. Where and when was the last one you took?
5. Would you have the courage to ask a celebrity to take a selfie with you?
6. 📶 Find the Ellen DeGeneres selfie. Why do you think it was retweeted so many times?

> I'd never have the courage. I'm way too shy to ask a celebrity for a selfie!

♪ I guess I took a good selfie, Let me take a selfie

4 Grammar: Narrative tenses

A Read the grammar box and match examples a–d with rules 1–4.

> **Past narration: simple, continuous, and perfect tenses**
>
> When telling a story, use a variety of tenses to sequence events logically:
>
> a Ellen took her phone out of her pocket and **went** into the audience. (past simple)
> b The photo was taken while she **was hosting** the show. (past continuous)
> c Later she announced that the photo **had crashed** Twitter®. (past perfect)
> d Ellen was tired because she **had been working** really hard. (past perfect continuous)
>
> 1 [d] : longer action in progress before the time of a new event
> 2 [ ] : longer action in progress at the same time as a new event
> 3 [ ] : two single or short events that happened at the same time
> 4 [ ] : a single or short event before the time of a new event

>> **Grammar expansion p. 142**

B Circle the most logical way to complete five people's reactions to the show.
1 I thought the Oscars were a bit boring, so I [**turned** / **had turned**] off the TV and went to bed.
2 I could hardly recognize some of the actors! They [**had changed** / **had been changing**] a lot.
3 Ellen was the best host I [**had seen** / **had been seeing**] in years! She did a wonderful job.
4 When they took the selfie, I [**hadn't paid** / **wasn't paying**] attention. Too bad I missed it!
5 When the show finally ended, I [**was sleeping** / **had been sleeping**] for hours!

C Read *Spoken grammar*. Then rewrite the underlined sentences in tweets 1–4 to make the grammar traditional.

> **Spoken grammar**
>
> Here are three traditional grammar rules that people sometimes break in informal spoken English:
> 1 Avoid continuous forms with stative verbs, such as *like*, *need*, and *want*.
> 2 Use the past perfect after "It was the first second / third / time … "
> 3 Use the past perfect continuous for earlier actions when you say how long they were in progress.

1 I bet Ellen <u>had been wanting</u> *(wanted)* to host the show for a long time. Good for her.
2 Hated the show. <u>It was the first time I saw it</u>. First and last.
3 Ellen said that <u>people were tweeting for half an hour</u> when the site crashed.
4 <u>I was really liking</u> the show at first until I saw that dumb selfie!

D Complete the text with the verbs in the correct tense.

This photo was taken on Einstein's 72nd birthday in 1951, while he ¹ _____ (return) from an event that ² _____ (take place) in his honor.

Einstein ³ _____ (just / get) into his car to go home when photographer Arthur Sasse ⁴ _____ (ask) him to smile for the camera.

It ⁵ _____ (be) a long day and Einstein was exhausted. But Sasse wouldn't give up. Einstein finally ⁶ _____ (agree), but stuck out his tongue. The photo became a cultural icon!

E Make it personal Share a selfie (or recent photo) and tell the story behind it. Which is the class favorite? Think through these three questions:
- The event: When did it happen? Where were you? What were you doing?
- Background: What had just happened? What had you been doing?
- The aftermath: What happened after the event? Why do you think you still remember it?

> This is me right here … This photo was taken in 2014, and I was 17 at the time. I had just graduated from high school.

3.3 What invention can't you live without?

5 Reading

A ▶ 3.8 Read the blog quickly and check (✔) the meaning of *serendipity*.

☐ The ability to make logical connections.
☐ Something good that happens by accident.
☐ Scientists' ability to create new inventions.

BLOGADMIN **THE POWER OF SERENDIPITY**

A lot of the things we buy, eat, and drink today were not designed and created step by step. Here are two examples of chance discoveries you might be unaware of.

If potato chips are ruining your diet, blame it on chef George Crum. According to one legend that became popular after Crum's death, in the 1850s, he had an impossible customer who kept sending his French fries back to the kitchen because they were "not crunchy enough." Eventually, Crum got sick and tired of the customer's never-ending complaints and decided to ignore all the dos and don'ts of potato frying: He sliced the potatoes extra thin, fried them in hot oil, and drowned them in salt. To his surprise, the customer, completely unaware of the changes, loved the new recipe and kept going back, again and again. Before long, Crum's fries became the house specialty, changing the history of junk food forever!

Speaking of food ... sometimes all you need to make a groundbreaking discovery is a snack. In the early 1940s, American engineer Percy Spencer was conducting an experiment to generate microwaves – a form of electromagnetic radiation – when he felt an odd sensation in his pants. Spencer reached for his pocket and found out that the chocolate bar he'd been saving for later had melted. He then tried to replicate the same experiment with popcorn – sure enough, it worked. A few years later, Spencer gave us the first microwave oven, which weighed 750 pounds and cost between $2,000 and $3,000. Little did he know that one day, his invention would become one of the most widely used household appliances in the whole world.

Some scientists and inventors are understandably reluctant to report accidental discoveries out of fear that they might appear foolish. Fair enough, but I can't help wondering, though, how many other discoveries and inventions we would have if all of us were more willing to admit that necessity isn't always the mother of invention and that serendipity does seem to play a major role in innovation. What do you think?

B Check (✔) the correct statement in each group. Which story did you enjoy more?

Crum ...
☐ was surprised by his customer's feedback on the new chips.
☐ invented a very popular story about a customer.

Spencer ...
☐ knew the microwave oven would become very popular.
☐ suspected that the microwaves might pop the corn.

C What's the writer's main point in the last paragraph? Do you agree?
☐ If we were more open-minded about serendipity, we might have many more good inventions.
☐ If we focused more on necessity, we would have more good inventions.

D ▶ 3.9 Look at the highlighted words in the blog and choose the correct alternatives. Listen to check.
1 *Crunchy* sounds like a [**positive** / **negative**] adjective to describe [**food** / **places**].
2 *Slice* probably describes a way of [**cutting** / **cooking**] food.
3 *Groundbreaking* sounds like a [**positive** / **negative**] adjective that describes [**minor** / **major**] events.
4 *Odd* sounds like a [**positive** / **negative**] adjective.
5 *Widely* is an adverb that probably describes [**frequency** / **size**].

E **Make it personal** Choose one item from each pair that you couldn't live without. Compare in groups. Can you change everyone's mind?

bed / sofa   fridge / air conditioning   microwave / stove
buses / trains fruit / vegetables   wide-screen TV / tablet

> I'd die without a microwave. I don't know how to cook!

♪ You could be my luck. Even in a hurricane of frowns, I know that we'll be safe and sound

3.3

6 Vocabulary: Binomials

A Read *Binomials*. Then scan paragraphs 1 and 2 of the blog in **5A** and complete the chart with the bold expressions.

> **Binomials**
>
> Remember that binomials are expressions where two words are joined by a conjunction, most frequently "and." The word order is usually fixed. Binomials may have:
> 1 Repeated words: *I've never met a famous scientist* **face to face** *(in person).*
> 2 Combined opposites: *What are the* **pros and cons** *(advantages and disadvantages) of microwave cooking?*
> 3 Combined related words: *Creativity is the* **heart and soul** *(essence) of successful businesses.*

1 fed up _sick and tired_	3 done in stages _____
2 repeatedly _____	4 rules _____

> **Common mistake**
>
> I'm sick and tired ~~to eat~~ *of eating* junk food. I need some vegetables for a change!

B ▶ 3.10 Use your intuition to complete these song lines. Listen to check.
1 "If you fall, I will catch you. I'll be waiting, **time after** _time_ ." (Cindy Lauper)
2 "We've had some fun, and yes, we've had our **ups and** _____ ." (Huey Lewis and The News)
3 "It's not the game; it's how you play. And if I fall, I get up again, **over and** _____ ." (Madonna)
4 "**Sooner or** _____ , we learn to throw the past away." (Sting)
5 "For **better or** _____ , till death do us part, I'll love you with every beat of my heart, I swear." (All4one)
6 "Every **now and** _____ I get a little bit tired of listening to the sound of my tears." (Bonnie Tyler)
7 "You've got a friend in me when the road looks rough ahead, and you're **miles and** _____ from your nice warm bed. You've got a friend in me." (Randy Newman)

C ▶ 3.11 Listen to two friends and answer the questions.
1 How did Ann start dating her boyfriend?
2 Where did she know him originally?

D ▶ 3.11 Listen again. Write down the six binomials Ann uses. Check **AS** 3.11 on p.162. Do you have a favorite word in English, like Ann?

E **Make it personal** In groups, share good things that have happened to you by accident. Use at least one binomial. Does the whole class believe serendipity is both real and powerful?

winning money unexpectedly
meeting old friends / your soulmate
near misses
a lucky find
an amazing coincidence
an accidental / fortunate discovery
following your intuition successfully

> I had an amazing experience last month! I'd just left home for work when all of a sudden … and …

3.4 What was your favorite activity as a child?

7 Listening

A ▶ 3.12 Read the webpage and check (✔) the meaning of *fad*. Then listen to a conversation. Which fad from the website are they talking about?

A fad is something that ...
- ☐ is really fun and enjoyable.
- ☐ wastes people's time.
- ☐ is very popular for just a short time.

I MISS THAT FAD — Our favorite fads from years past! What are yours?

2000s

High school Musical
Every teenager's dream; every parent's nightmare.

Oversized sunglasses
For those who want to be noticed.

MP3 players
Yes, people didn't always use their phones!

2010s

Psy's Gangnam Style dance moves
Biggest YouTube hit ever.

Angry Birds
A cell-phone game with over 500m downloads!

Photo bombing
The art of sabotaging people's photos.

B ▶ 3.12 Listen again. T (true) or F (false)?
1. The fad was very popular in Joe's class.
2. He didn't want the teacher to see what he was doing.
3. He never played at home.
4. He usually played with friends.
5. He lost his enthusiasm after a while.

C ▶ 3.13 Write the missing letters. Listen carefully. How are the sounds pronounced?

JOE: I was crazy about [beep], you know. Actu*a*lly, everyone in my class, boys and girls, _sed to love it.
PEDRO: Oh, yeah?
JOE: Uh huh. It was such an _bsessi_n. I used t_ sit in the back row so the teacher w_ _ldn't see me. Then I'd get home from school, l_ck myself in my r_ _m, and start again, playing the same game over and over.
PEDRO: S_ _nds b_ring.
JOE: No, it was fun, actu_lly, though a bit s_l_tary. I'd spend hours and hours alone, trying to get r_d of the pigs. I j_st kept playing the same game again and again.
PEDRO: How good were you?
JOE: I was OK, I guess. Well, eventu_lly I beg_n to use it less and less … , and then I just del_ted th_ app from my phone.

D Re-read the conversation in **C** and underline the evidence supporting 1–5 in **B**.

E Make it personal In pairs, answer 1–4. Anything in common?
1. Are you familiar with the fads in **A**? Which ones are still popular?
2. Can you think of any other fads, past or present?
3. If you could bring a fad back from an earlier time, which would it be?
4. Which would you love to kill off forever?

> Oh, I'd get rid of those stupid online contests – like the ice-bucket challenge that was so popular a few years back.

♪ I used to rule the world. Seas would rise when I gave the word. Now in the morning I sleep alone. Sweep the streets I used to own

3.4

8 Grammar: Describing past habits and states

A Read the grammar box and complete the chart for *used to*.

> **Past habits and states: simple past, *used to*, and *would***
>
> a Once I **got** a Tamagotchi for my birthday. I **played** with it every single day. I really **liked** it. (simple past)
> b **I didn't use to / never used to** collect DVDs. (*used to*)
> c I **used to** have really long hair. I**'d** spend hours combing it. (*used to* and *would*)

We often start with *used to* and then continue with *would*. Past tenses can express:	a single action	a habit	a state
simple past	✔	✘	✔
used to			
would	✘	✔	✘

>> Grammar expansion p.142

Common mistakes
In the 90s, ~~it~~ (there) used to be a show on TV called *Dinosaurs*. It ~~would~~ (was / used to be) very popular.

B Read about two more fads. Which verbs in **bold** can be replaced by *used to*? Have you ever tried these or similar fashion fads?
In the 60s, straight hair used to be very fashionable.

Don't be alarmed by the photo – there's a logical explanation! In the 60s, straight hair **was** very fashionable. Teenagers all over **would spend** hours and hours ironing their hair, trying to look their best! Thank goodness for modern technology. Today's hair straighteners are much safer!

Bellbottoms **became** extremely popular in the 60s, partly because artists like Elvis Presley and James Brown **would wear** them in their shows, night after night. Also, in the 70s, hippies **saw** bell-shaped pants as a way to rebel against their parents. Bellbottoms **came back** a few years ago and haven't completely disappeared. Are there any in your closet?

9 Pronunciation: Weak form of *and*; *used* vs. *used to*

A ▶ 3.13 Listen to 7C again. Notice the links and the pronunciation of *and* (/n/).

boys and girls   over and over   hours and hours   again and again   less and less

B ▶ 3.14 Pronounce *used to* with /s/, not /z/. Which do you hear? Write "s" or "z."
1 _s_ I used to have an MP3 player.
2 ___ We used that book in class last year.
3 ___ My mom used to play that game over and over.
4 ___ Have you ever used a PlayStation?

C Make it personal Did you have a childhood ob**ses**sion? In groups, share your stories.
- How old were you at the time?
- How did your obsession start?
- How often did you use to do it?
- How long did it last? When did you lose your en**thus**iasm?

> I used to be crazy about *Friends*. I'd spend hours and hours watching *Friends* reruns.

3.5 What makes you really happy?

10 Listening

A ▶ 3.15 What do you think makes these people happy? Listen and fill in the missing words.

1 Getting good _____ on my _____

3 Learning how to _____ _____ _____

2 Spending _____ _____ with my child

4 Enjoying life's _____ _____

B ▶ 3.15 Listen again. Note down one reason for each person's answer.

11 Keep talking

A ▶ 3.16 Competition! In teams, complete each quote with one word. Listen to check. Which team guessed the most words correctly?

1 "For every minute you are _angry_, you lose sixty seconds of happiness." (Ralph Waldo Emerson)
2 "Happiness is not something ready-made. It comes from your own _____." (Dalai Lama)
3 "Joy is not in _____; it is in us." (Richard Wagner)
4 "One of the keys to happiness is a bad _____." (Rita Mae Brown)
5 "If you spend your whole life waiting for the storm, you'll never enjoy the _____." (Morris West)
6 "The true way to make ourselves happy is to love our _____ and find in it our pleasure." (Madame de Motteville)

B Which is your favorite quote and why?   *I love number 4. If you think about ... too often, you can't enjoy it.*

C **Make it personal** In groups, answer 1–5 and compare your choices. You can't say "both" or "It depends." Can you change anyone's mind?

What do you really need to be happy?

1 a very high IQ or very good looks
2 a loving family or a circle of very close friends
3 a well-paid job or a job you love
4 luck or persistence
5 perfect health and not enough money or less-than-perfect health and lots of money

I think a high IQ is much more important. Looks are temporary; IQ is permanent!

D In pairs, complete this sentence in as many ways as you can.

My idea of perfect happiness is ...

My idea of perfect happiness is having a long weekend lunch with my family.

Clap along if you feel like a room without a roof (Because I'm happy). Clap along if you feel like happiness is the truth

12 Writing: Telling a story (1)

A Read Bob's story and complete the first sentence with a choice from 11C. Do you identify with his story?

WHAT DO YOU REALLY NEED TO BE HAPPY?

This week's winner: Bob Goldman, from Chicago

Last year I made a decision that completely changed my life and taught me that in order to be really happy all you need is _____ .

I come from a family of well-respected lawyers who had always expected me to follow in their footsteps. Day after day, Mom and Dad would spend hours talking about cases they'd won, trials they'd attended, and people they'd helped – just to get me interested in law. *Eventually*, they were able to persuade me to go to law school.

Initially, I enjoyed my classes, but *after a while*, I realized that law was probably not for me. I started missing classes, and my grades kept getting worse and worse. *In the meantime*, a friend who had a small band invited me to be the bass player, and I jumped at the chance. We played mostly at weddings and birthday parties, usually on the weekends, but it was wonderful.

One day, *as* we were packing up after a gig, a man who had come to see us several times introduced himself as an agent. He said he loved our music, and he offered us a record deal – just like that! *Suddenly*, it all made sense: Music, not law, was my destiny. So I quit law school, got into music school, and continued playing with the band on a part-time basis. I know I might only make half as much money as I would as a lawyer, but I don't care. I followed my heart, and I'm happier than I've ever been.

B Write *Do* or *Don't* at the beginning of guidelines 1–4.

When you write a narrative …

1 __do__ include at least three paragraphs.
2 _____ try to build suspense.
3 _____ reveal the main event right in the first paragraph.
4 _____ include enough background information.

C Read *Write it right!* Then find and match the highlighted linking words in the story to the synonyms in the chart.

Write it right!

When you are writing a story, use linking words, such as *at first*, *while*, and *immediately*, to make the sequence of events clear and build interest and suspense.

Sequencing		
1 at first	2 some time later	3 finally
a _initially_	b _____	c _____
Simultaneous events		**Interruptions**
4 while	5 meanwhile	6 all of a sudden
d _____	e _____	f _____

D ▶ 3.17 Improve these extracts from other competition entries by adding two linking words from 1–6 in **C** to each. Then do the same for a–f. Listen to some sample answers. Did you choose the same words?

1 We moved to London in 2010. *At first* I hated the neighborhood, our house, and my new school. *Some time later*, I began to change my mind, though, little by little.

2 I was on my way back home from work, my phone rang, and I got the best news ever: My wife had just had twins! I realized that our lives had changed forever.

3 I lost my job last year and spent months looking for a new one. I started learning another language to increase my chances. I found the job of my dreams, but it took a long time.

E Your turn! Write your own competition entry in about 200 words.

Before

Pick an item from 11C and think of a story that illustrates your choice.

While

Check the guidelines in **B** and use at least four linking words from **C**.

After

Proofread, especially the tenses. Share your story with the class. Which one should win the competition?

Are you ever deceived by ads?

1 Vocabulary: False advertising

A Read the guide. In pairs, share five tips to protect yourself from false ads.

> I haven't stayed in a hotel in years. Can you recognize a fake review?

> Yes ... if it doesn't give many details, it's probably fake.

Common mistake
Our hotel was filthy! What a ~~deception~~ *disappointment*!

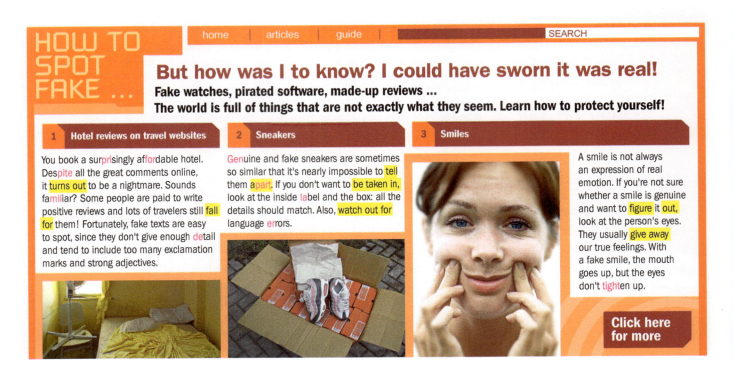

B ▶ 4.1 Complete dictionary entries 1–7 with the highlighted phrasal verbs in the correct form. Listen to check.

Separable:
1. reveal something secret: "I can't lie. My voice always __gives__ me __away__."
2. passive when meaning to fool or deceive someone: "I've never _____ by a TV ad."
3. recognize the difference between two people or things: "The twins look so much alike that no one can _____ them _____."
4. discover an answer or solve a problem: "It took me weeks to _____ how to use our new washing machine."

Inseparable:

5. look out or be on the alert for: "What problems should I _____ when buying a used car?"
6. be deceived by something: "I can't believe you _____ that trick!"
7. prove to be the case in the end: "This jacket was cheap, but it _____ to be really warm."

C ▶ 4.2 Re-read and listen to the guide in A. Then use only the photos to remember at least three tips. Use phrasal verbs.

> If you look at the shoe label, you won't be taken in.

♪ You can't judge a sister by looking at her brother. You can't judge a book by looking at the cover

4.1

D Complete the next item in the guide with phrasal verbs from **B**.

E Make it personal In groups, choose a topic from those below. What information would you include in a "how to spot" guide?

HOW TO SPOT ...
- fake discounts and special offers
- suspicious emails
- fake friends

4 Facebook® profiles

Be careful before accepting friend requests from strangers. You might be _____ . Studies suggest that there may be more than 100 million fake Facebook® accounts worldwide. Here are two signs that can _____ a fake profile and help you _____ if you're talking to a real person:

- Pages with few status updates, but lots of "likes," often _____ to be fake.
- You can also _____ real and fake profiles _____ because the average Facebook® user has over 300 friends. An impostor will often have far fewer.

> Let's see ... how about this: Emails from banks sometimes turn out to be viruses.

> Yeah. And watch out for other signs too, like spelling mistakes.

2 Listening

A ▶ 4.3 Listen to Kim, Mark, and Linda talking about fake goods. Which ways to identify a fake product can you infer? Check (✔) the correct answers.

Fake goods ...
1. ☐ often come without the original packaging.
2. ☐ are often more affordable.
3. ☐ don't always work well.
4. ☐ can't always be returned.

B ▶ 4.4 Listen to the rest of the conversation. What does Mark want to do with his phone? Does Kim agree in the end?

C ▶ 4.4 Listen again and order their arguments against fake goods 1–4. Can you think of any others?

Fake goods ...
- ☐ may harm the environment.
- ☐ might discourage new products.
- ☐ could hurt the country's economy.
- ☐ are made under bad working conditions.

> Fake goods can be expensive. You think you're saving, but they don't last.

D Make it personal Try to persuade the class!

1 ▶ 4.5 **How to say it** Complete the sentences. Then listen to check.

Developing an argument (2)	
What they said	What they meant
1 Just because (it's legal) doesn't _____ (it's ethical).	Being (legal) doesn't make it (ethical).
2 _____ you'd agree that ...	I know you'd also agree that ...
3 You're _____ the point.	You don't understand my argument.
4 Let me _____ it another way.	Let me make the same point differently.
5 Look at it this _____ .	Listen to my (convincing) argument.

2 Choose a dilemma from the list on the right, or think of your own, and note down arguments for or against.

3 In groups, present your arguments. Who was the most convincing?

Is it ever acceptable to ...
- use a radar detector?
- cheat at sports?
- take someone's photo without permission?
- genetically modify food?
- break the law to save someone's life?
- lie on your résumé?

> I think it's wrong to use a radar detector while you're driving. I'm not sure it's illegal, though.

> Yeah, just because you can use one doesn't mean you should.

4.2 Are teachers important in the digital age?

3 Language in use

A 🔊 ▶ 4.6 Read the homepage. Then listen to / watch a teacher and circle the correct alternatives.

This week's

Fact or Fiction:

"Flipped classrooms": Do students actually learn better?

FIRST THINGS FIRST: WHAT IS "FLIPPED LEARNING"?

It's an approach to education where students learn content at home mostly by [watching video lectures / reading articles], and homework is done in class through [taking weekly tests / discussion and problem-solving].

What do you think? Would flipped learning work for *you*?

Click here to watch a flipped classroom in action.

B In pairs, are / were your science lessons like that?

> My physics teacher was horrendous. I used to fall asleep.

C Read the comments on a discussion forum and predict the missing words 1–5 from the box. There are two extra words.

| coffee | communication | ~~focus~~ | grades | language | sleep | smile |

1 Location: Australia Learning through video at home might be enjoyable. But in spite of all the fun, it would take a lot of self-discipline and _focus_ not to check my Twitter® feed or upload a photo to Instagram® every five minutes.

2 Location: U.S. I'd definitely miss having live lectures. I think my _____ and test scores might improve, though, since I'd be able to watch all the explanations again and again, go at my own speed, stop, drink coffee, take notes …

3 Location: Brazil Despite its advantages, "flipped learning" wouldn't work for me. I need a real live teacher to _____ at me, nod, look me in the eye … you know, just generally encourage me.

4 Location: Mexico Although "flipped learning" is becoming very popular and even though it might work well for math and science, I think "hands-on" skills should be taught traditionally. I mean, just imagine what it would be like to learn how to drive like that. Or to learn a _____ !

5 Location: Canada Absolutely. Unlike other subjects, languages should be learned through _____ – and preferably in the country where they're spoken.

D Answer 1–4 in groups. Any disagreements?
1 Who do you agree with?
2 Can you think of another (dis)advantage?
3 Do you think there should be a minimum age for "flipped learning"?
4 Would you like to learn English in a flipped classroom?

> I think it would be fun. Plus, we'd have more time to speak in class.

> I don't know … I hate spending too long in front of a screen.

♪ School's out for summer. School's out forever. School's been blown to pieces

4 Grammar: Conjunctions to compare and contrast ideas

A Read the examples. Then check (✔) the correct grammar rules a–c.

Conjunctions: *although, (even) though, despite, in spite of, unlike, while,* and *whereas*

Comparing
1 **Unlike** my classmates, I can't stand the "flipped" classroom.
2 My grades improved **while** my sister's stayed the same.
3 Teenagers can learn independently **whereas** small children need more guidance.

Conceding (but …)
4 **Although / (Even) though** the students work at home, the teacher is still essential.
5 Learning on your own is practical. It can be a bit lonely, **though**.
6 Some people are still skeptical **despite / in spite of** the good results.
7 **Despite / In spite of** having a bad Internet connection, I still manage to do my homework.

a **Though** can come at the end of a sentence. ☐
b Use the *-ing* form or a noun phrase after **despite / in spite of**. ☐
c Use a complete sentence after **while** and **whereas**. ☐

Common mistake

the fact that it is convenient
Despite ~~it is convenient~~, online learning is not for me.

B In pairs, rephrase the examples (1–7) in the grammar box using *but*.

» Grammar expansion p.144

> OK, number 1: I can't stand the "flipped classroom," but my classmates like it.

C Read the opinions on comment 5 in 3C. Circle the correct words. Which ones do you agree with?

1 **Location: Peru**   I agree you need to spend some time abroad to master a language. Or marry a native! Lots of people, of course, disagree with me, [**though / although**].
2 **Location: Colombia**   Well, I disagree. Have you heard of that guy who's fluent in 11 languages [**although / despite**] he's never left his country? How do you explain that?
3 **Location: India**   I'd say he's exaggerating. But I speak fluent French [**even though / in spite of**] the fact that I've never been to France or Canada.
4 **Location: U.S.**   How about the opposite? Take my grandma. [**Unlike / Whereas**] my grandpa, she speaks very poor English [**even though / despite**] she's lived in the U.S. for nearly forty years.
5 **Location: Japan**   Well, [**while / in spite of**] there are exceptions, I still think you need to be surrounded by the language 24/7 to become truly fluent.

> Well, I'm not sure. Although some people say you can only learn a language abroad, I actually think …

D Make it personal   In groups, can you think of misconceptions usually associated with the topics below? Search online for "popular misconceptions" for more ideas. Use conjunctions!

controversial celebrities   health and fitness   kids' beliefs   current events   intelligence   sleeping

> Although some say we need eight hours of sleep every night, I've read it's not necessarily true.

> It really varies. … whereas …

> Even though some believe …

> Despite what many kids are told …

> People think … That's not necessarily true, though.

> Unlike most of us, I actually think …

4.3 What was the last rumor you heard?

5 Reading

A In pairs, read the first part of the article, a paragraph at a time. Answer the questions in bold. Then read the next paragraph to check.

MY COUSIN'S NEIGHBOR SWEARS HE SAW IT TOO!

1. If you're planning a visit to New York City any time soon, be careful if you use the subway. It's filled with danger. **"What kind of danger?"** you must be wondering.

2. The kind that purses are made of. Apparently, the sewers under the city are filled with mutant alligators, waiting for their next victim. Back in the day, southern migrants moved to New York City and took their pet alligators (!) with them. At first, it seemed like a good idea, but in the end, Manhattan and alligators turned out to be a bad match. So some owners got tired of their pets and simply dumped them into the city's sewers. They started multiplying, of course, and, in no time, formed an underground city of reptiles. **Now, why would anybody fall for a story like that?**

3. Oh, human nature, I guess. Although it seems logical that underground Manhattan wouldn't be hospitable to cold-blooded reptiles, this particular urban legend, like many others, refuses to go away. In the process of writing my latest book, *What if it turns out to be true?* I tried to figure out why these myths persist. But first things first: **What exactly is an urban legend?**

4. It's like a modern-day fairy tale, except it's retold as a true story and usually includes an element of fear. An urban legend tends to spread very quickly. All it takes is one person to share it with someone else and, soon enough, it's all over the Internet. These are some common questions people ask about urban legends.

B Read the second part. Match the questions and answers. There's one extra question.

a Why do people create urban legends?
b How do urban legends originate?
c Are all urban legends false?
d Do all cultures have urban legends?

5. _Are all urban legends false_ ?
Nine times out of ten, that turns out to be the case. However, some urban legends are based on actual events that are changed and exaggerated so much that, at some point, they become fictional stories with bits of truth in them – pretty much like some of today's journalism. New versions of classic legends also appear from time to time, which means they're never out of date.

6. _____?
Experts think they do, although since urban legends are often passed on as stories that "happened to a friend," it's virtually impossible to trace them back to their original source. Most people, though, tend to enjoy these stories for what they are – stories – and don't ask their origin because they know they're being taken in.

7. _____?
To me, this is perhaps the most intriguing question. While we don't know the reasons exactly, we do know that urban legends are an integral part of popular culture. They represent who we are as a society and reflect our own concerns and fears. Plus, as my grandmother used to say, "Life is much more interesting if there are monsters in it." I couldn't agree more.

C ▶ 4.7 Re-read and listen to both parts. In which paragraphs (1–7) are these points made? Did you enjoy the article?

- [4] Urban legends spread rapidly and are often meant to make people afraid.
- [ ] Some urban legends make no sense, but they remain popular.
- [ ] Some of today's news stories are not very reliable.
- [ ] Urban legends make our lives more exciting.
- [ ] People like urban legends even though they suspect they might be fake.

D Make it personal 🌐 Do you know the two urban legends below? Search online for more "urban legends".

> There's that one about the hitchhiker that disappears. Or is that a movie?

> I heard that if you leave a tooth in a glass of soda overnight, it will completely dissolve!

Common mistake

heard
Last week I ~~listened~~ Katy Perry had retired. It turned out to be a rumor.

♪ It took me by surprise I must say. When I found out yesterday. Don't you know that I heard it through the grapevine

4.3

6 Vocabulary: Time expressions

A ▶ 4.8 Listen and match three conversations to pictures a–c. Which was the easiest to understand? Why?

B ▶ 4.9 Complete parts of conversations 1–3 with the highlighted expressions in the article in 5A and B. Listen to check.

1 A: _At first_ (= initially), I wasn't sure whether the story was real.
   B: ... So I guess _____ (= it turned out that), Don was lying.
2 A: Well, _____ (= in the past), people used to say that taking a shower after a meal could kill you.
   B: I eat and then shower _____ (= occasionally) – maybe once a month – and I'm still here.
3 A: Try refreshing the page. Maybe it's _____ (= not updated).
   B: Oh, don't worry! _____ (= sooner or later) we're going to find out that the rumors are false.
   A: You post something and, _____ (= very quickly), it's all over the web.

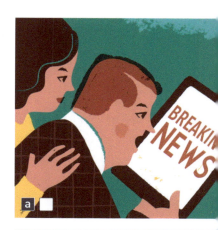
a

C Make it personal In groups, make true statements with four of the expressions in B. Whose were the most interesting?

> Last week, I was walking home when ... At first ...

b

D ▶ 4.10 Read *Similes*. Then match the words in the circles. There are three extra words or phrases in circle 3. Listen to check.

Similes

Using a verb + *like* + a noun can make your descriptions more vivid:
I was so scared (that) **I ran like the wind.** (= very fast)
This dress **fits like a glove**. (= fits perfectly)
Remember: These are fixed combinations. You can't change the words!

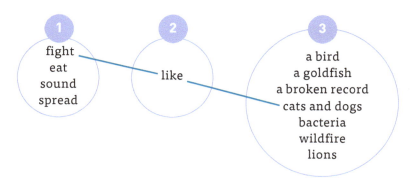

c

E Using only the pictures and new expressions, improvise and expand the three mini dialogs in B.

> Have you lost your mind? You can't throw a coin from here.

> Why not? They say it brings good luck ...

F Make it personal In groups, answer 1–2. Anything in common?

1 Do you ever check if a news story is true before you share it on social media?
2 Are you into gossip? Have you ever accidentally spread a false rumor?

> I'm really into celebrity gossip. I love expressions like "A little bird told me (that) ..."

4.4 How would you describe yourself?

7 Listening

A ▶ 4.11 Listen to Bill and Rachel on a radio show describing an experiment. Order the pictures 1–3.

B ▶ 4.11 Listen again. T (true) or F (false)?
1 The experiment was designed to sell a product.
2 After each woman described herself, the artist drew her.
3 He then drew a second sketch looking at the woman.
4 The participants had all met before the show.

C ▶ 4.12 Guess the experiment results. Circle *more* or *less*. Listen to check. Any surprises?

BILL: As it turns out, the <mark>sketches</mark> based on self-descriptions were [**more** / **less**] attractive than the other drawings – all of them! In other words, when participants were asked to describe each other, they were [**more** / **less**] positive than when they talked about themselves.

RACHEL: Well, I'm not surprised, really.

BILL: I was a bit <mark>puzzled</mark> myself, to be honest. Anyway, the moral of the story is that maybe you're [**more** / **less**] attractive than you give yourself credit for.

RACHEL: Yeah. In other words, how we <mark>see</mark> ourselves is one thing; how others view us, quite another.

D Read *Avoiding repetition*. Then connect the <mark>highlighted</mark> words in **C** to their (near) synonyms.

> **Avoiding repetition**
>
> Writers often use (near) synonyms to avoid repetition. When you come across an unknown word, look for related words nearby. They can help you guess the meaning!
>
> This experiment was **conducted** by a New York psychologist. It was **carried out** to change the way people see themselves.

E **Make it personal** In pairs, choose three questions to discuss. Are your answers similar?
1 Do you remember what product was being advertised? Was this a good experiment for it?
2 What do you think might have happened if they'd picked men instead of women?
3 What's your favorite recent photo of yourself? Why? Who has seen it?
4 Do others usually see you the same way you see yourself?
5 Has your personality / self-image changed much as you've grown older?

> My friends say I'm really outgoing, but I think I'm a bit shy, actually.

> I don't think you're shy at all.

♪ One life, With each other, Sisters. Brothers. One life ... We get to carry each other

4.4

8 Grammar: Reflexive pronouns and *each other / one another*

A Read the grammar box. Then find an example of emphasis in 7C.

> **Reflexive pronouns with *-self / -selves*; reciprocal actions with *each other / one another***
>
> When the subject and object are the same person:
> 1 **We** can be too critical of **ourselves**.
>
> 2 For emphasis:
>   I **myself** was surprised by the results.
>   I was surprised by the results **myself**.
>
> 3 To express "all alone" or "without help":
>   **The artist** sketched the pictures **(by) himself**.
>
> 4 To express reciprocal actions:
>   **We** were asked to describe **each other** / **one another**.

» Grammar expansion p.144

B Do a) and b) have the same or a different meaning? In pairs, explain the differences.
1 The two politicians introduced **a) themselves b) each other**.
2 Before the debate, they had really motivated **a) themselves b) each other**.
3 They argued **a) a lot b) a lot with each other**.
4 We taught **a) ourselves b) one another** how to play the guitar.
5 My daughter wrote her name **a) herself b) by herself**.
6 The children drew pictures **a) by themselves b) of themselves**.

> In sentence a), the politicians say their own names, but in sentence b), they say the name of the other politician.

C ▶ 4.13 Read *Common mistakes*. Then check (✔) the correct pronouns in sentences 1–5 and change the wrong ones. Listen to check.

1 You see ~~yourself~~ in mirrors often, so your minds internalize that image. *yourselves*
2 If you see an ugly angle, you can instantly correct itself.
3 We stand closer to mirrors than to each other, so we see us from the same height.
4 When people see theirselves in a photo, their imperfections are magnified.
5 On some level, we will always be a mystery to ourselves. But maybe not to others!

> **Common mistakes**
> You can both put on your shoes ~~yourself~~. *yourselves.*
> Sarah and ~~myself~~ are going to the meeting. *I*
> I got ~~myself~~ up at six yesterday.
> The survivors consider ~~theirselves~~ fortunate. *themselves*

9 Pronunciation: Final /l/

A ▶ 4.14 Read about final /l/. Then listen and repeat 1 and 2.

> The /l/ at the end of a syllable or word is pronounced with the tongue further back in the mouth.
> 1 Paul, I don't see myself as a celebrity at all.
> 2 On some level, we will always be a mystery to ourselves.

B **Make it personal** In groups, answer 1–5. Then share the most surprising answers with the class. Remember to pronounce final /l/ carefully.

1 Do you like looking at yourself in the mirror, or do you look better in photos?
2 How often do you and your closest friends call / email / text each other?
3 Have you ever tried to teach yourself something? How successful were you?
4 What exactly is your usual morning routine? What are the first six things you do?
5 Have you ever formed a false perception of someone? What made you change it?

> Well, when I look at myself in the mirror, I look thin, but in photos I often look heavier.

4.5 How many pairs of glasses do you own?

10 Listening

A ▶ 4.15 Listen to Liz talking to her friend Ryan. Answer 1–3.
1 What's special about Liz's glasses?
2 Did she buy them herself?
3 Where were they made?

B ▶ 4.16 In pairs, guess six things the X29 can do. Listen and take notes. Any surprises?

> I never knew smart glasses could …
>
> Me neither. And I had no idea it was possible to …

C ▶ 4.16 Listen again. Check (✔) the correct answer.

It can be inferred that Liz …
1 ☐ speaks good Portuguese.
2 ☐ wishes the X29 was a better translator.
3 ☐ doesn't mind speaking in public.
4 ☐ exercises.

D ▶ 4.17 Listen to the end of the conversation. Order Liz's feedback 1–4. Which aspect(s) was she surprised by?

The glasses …
☐ can be socially isolating.
☐ make multitasking difficult.
☐ are a little uncomfortable to wear.
☐ are kind of unnatural in a way that's hard to explain.

E ▶ 4.18 Read *Figurative expressions with 'die'*. Then complete 1–3. Listen to check.

> **Figurative expressions with *die***
>
> You can use the verb *die* figuratively to emphasize your ideas:
>
> **I'm dying for / to get** a pair of smart glasses. (= I really want …)
> My mother's **scared to death** of technology. (= She's very afraid of …)
> **I wouldn't be caught dead** wearing that thing! (= I would never do it.)

1 I'm _____ ____ go to Rio de Janeiro.
2 I nearly _____ ____ embarrassment when my mind went blank.
3 The kids love them ____ _____ .

F Make it personal In pairs, answer 1–3. Any surprises?
1 Would you like to test the X29? Why?
2 What else do you think smart glasses should be able to do?
3 What other products would you volunteer to test?

> I'd love to test a 3D printer. I mean, that would be so cool!
>
> I'd never be a guinea pig for anything. I'd be too scared.

11 Keep talking

A Talk about a product that let you down. Think through 1–6 first.
1 Was it (a) a gift or (b) did you buy it yourself?
2 If (b), how did you choose it? Did you fall for a misleading ad / fake reviews?
3 Do you still have it? How much longer do you intend to keep it?
4 What are three things that turned out to be disappointing about this product?
5 Is / Was there anything positive about it? If so, what?
6 Would you recommend this product?

> Well, I once bought a new bicycle, and I regretted it immediately!

B In groups, share your stories. Who's had the worst experience?

♪ Don't tell me it's not worth trying for. You can't tell me it's not worth dying for. Everything I do, I do it for you

4.5

12 Writing: A product review

A Read Liz's review. Which feedback in **10D** has she changed her mind about?

B Re-read the review. Cross out the wrong guideline.

- Use headings to make your review easy to read.
- Start with an introduction.
- Use a very formal style.
- Try to find something positive to say, even if you don't like the product.
- Be careful to include only relevant details and information.
- Finish by saying whether or not you recommend the product.

C Read *Write it right!* Then underline five more similar expressions in the review.

> **Write it right!**
>
> Notice how the bold words and expressions can help you generalize:
> **As a rule**, the product worked well.
> Customer support was **generally** helpful.
> The experience was, **by and large**, satisfactory.
> The battery lasted five hours **on average**.

D Cross out the wrong alternatives, if any.
1. I read the manual and, on the whole, I found [it complicated / ~~a mistake on page 22~~].
2. Overall, my experience with your new 4D TV [was disappointing / started on Monday].
3. Generally speaking, the car [has a sunroof / handles great].
4. As a rule, I [don't write product reviews / didn't write a review of my last phone].
5. I've had the R34 for a week and, for the most part, [I'm disappointed / it works well].

E **Your turn!** Write a review of the product you talked about in **11A** in 175–200 words.

Before
Re-read questions 4–6 and think of any details you can add.

While
Check the guidelines in **B** and use at least four phrases from **C** to express generalizations.

After
Proofread your review. Share it with the class.

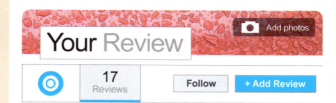

Rate the X29!

I've had the X29 for thirty days and, generally speaking, I find the device well built, reliable, and easy to use. The glasses work well as a translator and mini-teleprompter, and the battery life is better than I expected. I'm not sure, though, if they have made my life easier.

Comfort

On the whole, the glasses are surprisingly comfortable. Even though the first few days were tough, I soon got used to wearing them. My husband, on the other hand, never did – possibly because he wears prescription glasses.

Multitasking

For the most part, it's nearly impossible to carry on everyday activities such as driving – or even crossing the street – while actively using the device, which has often made me wonder what the whole point of the X29 is.

Look

Overall, the X29 is stylish and tasteful. However, the screen is way too big, and the device attracts a lot of stares, which makes me feel really uncomfortable. It's possible, of course, that people are still not used to smart glasses and that this will change in the future.

Conclusion

In general, I believe the X29 is a solid product that people who are interested in technology will enjoy. However, if you're a more casual user like me, stick to your phone – at least until an improved version is available.

> **Common mistake**
>
>   *had*
> I have ∧ this product for about a week and I love it.

47

Review 2
Units 3–4

1 Speaking

A Look at the photos on p.38.

1 Note down two questions for each, using the phrasal verbs below.

> be taken in   fall for   figure out   give away   tell apart   turn out   watch out for

2 Take turns giving advice.
   A Choose a photo. Ask your questions.
   B Give **A** suggestions on how to avoid being taken in.

> How can you tell apart fake sneakers and real ones?

> Well, if you don't want to be taken in, you should …

B **Make it personal** Choose three question titles from Units 3 and 4 to ask a partner. Ask at least three follow-up questions for each. What did you learn about each other?

> Do you get embarrassed easily?

> Yes! The other day, I had just arrived at school when …

C Search on "common embarrassing moments" and in groups, share a story about someone you know who's experienced one of them, using *used to*, *would*, or the simple past.

> My little brother always used to have food in his teeth!

2 Listening

A R2.1 Listen to a radio show on embarrassing incidents.
Put the events in order. Write an X for any events that aren't mentioned.
The caller …
- ☐ complains about her boss.
- ☐ explains how she feels.
- ☐ is thanked by her boss.
- ☐ breaks up with her boyfriend.
- ☐ apologizes.
- ☐ goes to her boss's office.
- ☐ is working on a deadline.

B **Make it personal** In pairs, have you or has anyone you know ever had a similar experience? Share your stories using the expressions below.

> all of a sudden   at first   finally   meanwhile   some time later   while

> You'll never believe what once happened to me! …

Review 2 3–4

3 Grammar

A Circle the correct forms of the verbs.

I ¹[used to leave / was leaving] work every day at 6:00 p.m., but that day I ²[had stayed / would stay] late to finish a project. So at 8:00 p.m. I ³[just left / had just left] work, but the snow ⁴[already fell / was already falling]. The buses ⁵[didn't run / weren't running], so my only choice was to take the subway. But unfortunately, I ⁶[had injured / was injuring] my ankle two weeks before. Since I ⁷[wasn't able to / am not able to] walk down stairs, I ⁸[decided / used to decide] to take a taxi. The snow ⁹[kept falling / would keep falling], and my feet ¹⁰[were freezing / froze]. Finally, a nice taxi driver ¹¹[would stop / stopped]. He ¹²[had stopped / was stopping] working for the day, but he ¹³[took / used to take] me home anyway.

B In pairs, rewrite the paragraph, without changing the meaning, using at least four of these conjunctions. How many verbs can you change also?

| although | despite | even though | in spite of | though | unlike | whereas | while |

Although I usually finished work every day at 6:00 p.m., that day …

4 Self-test

Correct the two mistakes in each sentence. Check your answers in Units 3 and 4. What's your score, 1–20?
1 Everyone was staring me because I glanced my watch in class.
2 Jean sounded like a broken cassette with that false rumor, but it spread like fire.
3 So then he hear a really loud noise, so he look around and opened the door.
4 Sometimes I'm really tired to study English and hate hearing my accent over and again.
5 I didn't used to like bellbottoms and use to always wear straight pants.
6 That program would be very popular, but personally, I don't like it.
7 They should consider theirselves lucky and do more to help each others.
8 John and myself are planning a trip, and maybe you'd both like to join us yourself.
9 I have this phone for a week, and for and large, I like it.
10 Whereas my little brother, I can't learn to swim, in spite of really trying.

5 Point of view

Choose a topic. Then support your opinion in 100–150 words, and record your answer. Ask a partner for feedback. How can you be more convincing?
a You think false advertising is a serious problem. OR
   You think, by and large, companies do a good job of advertising their products.
b You think everyone buys fake goods, and it's nice to save money. OR
   You think the purchase of fake items is truly unethical.
c You think urban legends can be fun and persist because everyone enjoys them. OR
   You think urban legends can do serious damage when people start to believe them.
d You think "flipped learning" is a wonderful idea. OR
   You think "flipped learning" is only the latest fad and just a way for teachers to do less work.

5
What's your biggest life decision so far?

1 Vocabulary: Adversity

A ▶ 5.1 What do you know about these people? Guess the missing words. Then listen to check. Were you close?

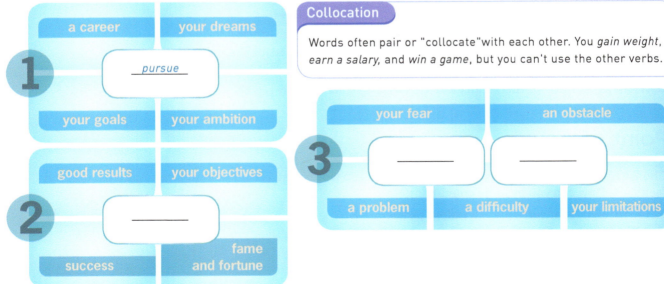

Against all odds

Three of my heroes! They fought ad**ver**sity, im**proved** our world, and taught me **val**uable lessons.

1. Albert Einstein is considered one of the _smartest_ people of all time, but he didn't have an easy _____. He didn't speak until he was _____ years old, and his teachers thought he was _____ and **ab**sent-minded. But he a**chieved** unbe**lie**vable _____ and eventually developed the **the**ory of _____.

2. It's hard to imagine the _____ industry without Oprah Winfrey. She over**came** extreme _____ and parental neglect to achieve fame and _____. After running away from _____ at the age of 14, she got her first job on TV at 19. And the rest is history. Her rare ability to connect with her _____ has made her the star she is today.

3. Dutch im**press**ionist painter Vincent van Gogh is considered one of the greatest _____ in history. What many people may not know is that he only sold one – yes, one – _____ during his short **life**time. He died in 1890 at the age of only 37. He **faced** many difficulties, and he made very little _____, but that didn't stop him from painting over 900 works of _____. He was a **tor**tured soul, but he just perse**vered** and pur**sued** his _____.

> I don't know very much about … yet. Was he/she the one who …

B Read *Collocation*. Then complete the mindmaps with the highlighted words in A.

1 _pursue_
- a career
- your dreams
- your goals
- your ambition

Collocation
Words often pair or "collocate" with each other. You *gain weight*, *earn a salary*, and *win a game*, but you can't use the other verbs.

2 _____
- good results
- your objectives
- success
- fame and fortune

3 _____ _____
- your fear
- an obstacle
- a problem
- a difficulty
- your limitations

C Which phrases from B can you use to describe 1) the people in A and 2) famous people from your own country?

> Let's see. Despite her family background, Oprah has achieved a lot of success.

♪ I can be your hero, baby. I can kiss away the pain

5.1

2 Listening

A ▶ 5.2 Read the webpage, listen to two people's stories, and complete the chart.

> # Our magazine is looking for heroes.
> ## Who are yours?
> They're your friends, neighbors, relatives – maybe even your parents. And their personal stories have in*spired* you and have had an *im*pact on your lives.
>
> **Share your story with us. Three questions to help you get started: Tara**
>
> 1. Who's your chosen hero?
> 2. What kind of problem has he / she been able to overcome?
>   ☐ health ☐ relationships ☐ money ☐ other (what?)
> 3. What did he / she do that so im*pressed* you?
>
> Send us a short video telling us about your hero.
>
> The ten most con*vin*cing entries will win a $1,000 gift card.

	Tara	Fernando
Speaker's relationship to ...	*friend*	
Problem(s)		
Most impressive thing		

B ▶ 5.2 Listen again. For each person, cross out the incorrect statement.

Tara ...	Fernando ...
couldn't afford her home.	is very close to his grandson.
didn't get along with her mom.	used to lead a stress-free life.
made a fortune on her first book.	had always been in good health.

C In pairs, whose story impressed you more? Why do you feel that way?

> Fernando's story really made a big impression on me because he never gave up.

D Make it personal For the webpage competition, who would you nominate as your own hero and why?

1. Think about questions 1–3 in **A** for two minutes. Read *Beginning a narrative*.
2. In groups, share ideas, and then take a vote. Which are the most convincing narratives? Whose story should win the prize?

> **Beginning a narrative**
>
> A good narrative creates suspense and gives only relevant details. Always start by capturing your listener's attention:
> *My cousin Bruno is amazing / unbelievable / a total inspiration!*

> My friend Sara is amazing! I'd like to nominate her. She's been in a wheelchair her whole life, but she ...

Common mistakes

My grandmother faced lots of setbacks, but she ~~overcome~~ *overcame* most of her problems and ~~turn~~ *turned* her life around. Don't forget! When you tell a story, be careful with both tense consistency and, in the present, third person -s.

5.2 What would you love to be able to do?

3 Listening

A Which skills (1–9) from the website have(n't) you learned?

NINE LIFESAVING SKILLS YOU'LL REGRET NOT LEARNING BEFORE YOU'RE 18!

1 cooking
2 driving
3 multitasking
4 playing a sport well
5 saving money
6 speaking a second language
7 learning self-defense
8 swimming
9 touch typing

> If only I could multitask!

> I haven't learned how to swim yet, and I'm already 16!

B ▶ 5.3 Listen to two colleagues. Which skill is Anthony talking about?

C ▶ 5.3 Listen again. T (true) or F (false)? Guess what they will say next.
1 Anthony was surprised he didn't pass.
2 He's taken the test four times this year.
3 Claire thinks instructors are usually friendly.
4 When Anthony had to turn, he got even more nervous.
5 There was an accident at the end of the test.

D ▶ 5.4 Complete the rest of the conversation with the sentences. Listen to check.

| I wish she wouldn't do that. | If only I'd started in my late teens. | I wish I knew, though. |

CLAIRE: Don't let it get you down. You can do it! You're taking lessons, right?
ANTHONY: Oh, yeah. It's been two years now.
CLAIRE: Two years? Wow! Same instructor?
ANTHONY: Yeah. She's all right. But she keeps yelling, "Watch out!" whenever I do something wrong. ¹_____ . It's really annoying.
CLAIRE: Why do you think you always get so nervous?
ANTHONY: No idea. ²_____ . If I did, I'd be able to do something about it. But here's the thing … I started taking lessons in my late 20s.
CLAIRE: So?
ANTHONY: Too late, I guess. ³_____ . For example, I still don't know how to park! Can you believe it?
CLAIRE: Look, just take the test again, and do the best you can. You'll do better next time.
ANTHONY: I don't think there will be a next time. After more than a hundred lessons and eight exams, I'm calling it quits. Enough is enough.
CLAIRE: Oh, no! Keep at it! It's never too late to learn.
ANTHONY: Maybe it's not meant to be.
CLAIRE: Don't be silly! Just stick with it.

E **Make it personal** Answer 1–4 in groups. Any big disagreements?
1 Guess how their conversation ends. Will Anthony retake the test?
2 If you were in Anthony's shoes, what would you do now?
3 Is it essential for adults to know how to drive?
4 Do you know anyone who took a long time to learn something? How about you?

> Well, if I was Anthony, I'd take a break and spend my money on something else.

♪ I, I wish you could swim like the dolphins. Like the dolphins can swim

5.2

4 Grammar: Imaginary situations (1)

A Match statements 1–3 to their meaning (a–c). Then check (✔) the correct rules.

Imaginary situations (1): *wish* and *If only*

1 **I wish I had started** when I was younger.
2 **If only I knew how** to park the car!
3 **I wish** my instructor **would give** clearer instructions.

a ☐ a strong wish for the present to be different
b ☐ a wish for the past to be different
c ☐ a wish for a situation or another person to change

For wishes about the present and future, we use a verb in the ☐ **simple present** ☐ **simple past**.
For regrets about the past, we use a verb in the ☐ **simple past** ☐ **past perfect**.

» Grammar expansion p.146

More about *wish*

Other verbs and tenses can also be used with *wish* to express the present or future:
I can't draw. → I wish I **could draw**.
He's coming with us. I don't like him. → I wish he **wasn't / weren't coming** with us.

The simple past and *would* are often interchangeable for repeated actions:
I wish my mom **listened** to me. = I wish my mom **would listen** to me.

Common mistake

I wish I ~~would~~ *could* speak French fluently.
Don't use *wish* or *if only* + *would* to talk about yourself.

B Choose the correct ending for sentences 1–3 in **A**.
1 ... but I [**don't / didn't**].   2 ... but I [**don't / didn't**].   3 ... but she [**doesn't / didn't**].

C ▶ 5.5   Complete six reactions to the website in **3A** with a subject and the correct verb form. Listen to check.
1 I wish _I knew_ (know) how to cook so I wouldn't spend so much on fast food.
2 I had the best dad in the world, but I wish _____ (teach) me how to save money.
3 Why are languages so hard? If only _____ (be) a magic pill to speak English.
4 Carlos, I wish _____ (miss) so many classes. Please try to come more often!
5 Mom says I'm not ready to get my driver's license yet. I wish _____ (change) her mind.
6 They say you can learn how to multitask at any age. If only _____ (be) true!

D Make it personal Role play "What went wrong?"

1 ▶ 5.6 **How to say it**   Complete the chart. Listen to check.

	Expressing encouragement	
	What they said	What they meant
1	Don't let it _____ you down.	Don't let it make you sad.
2	You'll _____ better next time.	Your performance will be better next time.
3	Do the _____ you can.	Try hard.
4	Keep _____ it!	Don't give up.
5	Stick _____ it!	Don't give up.

2 Role play in pairs. Explain what went wrong, and tell **B** two things you regret.

A Choose a situation.
an exam   a job interview   a sports event
a meal you cooked   an audition

So, how did it go?

B Support and encourage **A**, and ask for more details. Use *How to say it* expressions.

Terrible. I wish I'd studied more. I mean I couldn't even answer some questions.

5.3 How important is a college degree?

5 Reading

A In pairs, what can you learn about Victoria from the photo and title of the article? Then read the first paragraph to check. Were you close?

Up and coming
From dull dinosaurs to glorious Greek food

Meet Victoria Sánchez, the 25-year-old college dropout behind *Fossil*.

We all know the stories – talented individuals who didn't graduate from college, never regretted it, and still managed to make absurd amounts of money despite lots of setbacks. According to a recent survey, 63 of the 400 wealthiest people in the U.S. don't have a college degree. That's about one in six. *Up and coming* spoke to Victoria Sánchez, the archeology dropout behind *Fossil*, elected best Greek restaurant of the year.

Q: _Why archeology_____?
A: Mostly because I had a wonderful archeology teacher as a freshman. So I wanted to follow in her footsteps and pursue a career in science, as well.

Q: _____?
A: It took a while. I guess it wasn't until my sophomore year when it just hit me that there was life beyond dinosaurs and fossils and rocks. So at the end of the year, I dropped out, which hardly anyone in my family had done before. Since I knew that eventually I wanted an international career, I decided to spend some time traveling around Europe. That's when I fell madly in love with Greece.

Q: _____?
A: My friends couldn't believe their ears when I told them I'd decided to start my own business. But they were generally supportive – most of them, that is. They kept reminding me of all the famous dropouts who'd made a fortune, while secretly wondering, I think, if I had the skills to be my own boss. Mom was cool about it, too. She used to say, "Better to be stressed out and overworked than underpaid and unhappy." Dad wasn't exactly thrilled, though. He still wishes I'd stuck with archeology, even now! He's always had such an interest in it.

Q: _____?
A: Europe was great, but after that, being back home was pretty much the same since I had to study again! Before opening *Fossil*, I spent about a year reading about Greek cuisine, learning from experts, seeking mentors, and learning the basics of running a restaurant, which I knew virtually nothing about. Now I'm happier than I've ever been. *Fossil* is winning award after award, and we're opening our first restaurant abroad next month.

Q: _____?
A: Well, above all, I've learned that formal education, with its overemphasis on theory, doesn't necessarily lead to actual learning. Learning can take place at work with a boss mentoring you, by going abroad and immersing yourself in a new culture, while starting your own business – or in a million other ways. It's wrong to underestimate the power of practical, real-life experience.

Q: _____?
A: Well, I wouldn't go as far as that. For every mega-success, there are a thousand students who drop out of college and, after a few years, wish they hadn't. College can help you develop social skills, self-discipline, and good study habits. So, despite what some people might say, college is anything but a waste of time. In my case, though – and I don't want to generalize beyond my own experience – there were more effective ways to reach my goal.

B ▶ 5.7 Skim the interview to put the questions back in the article. Listen to check. Any difficult parts?

1 So are you saying that a college education is a complete waste of time?
2 What was life after college like?
3 How did people react when you broke the news?
4 When did you realize you'd had enough of college?
5 Why archeology?
6 Looking back, what have you learned from the whole experience?

C Read *Expressing negative ideas*. What does Victoria say to express 1–4? Underline the relevant sentences in **A**.

1 There were very few college dropouts in my family. _I dropped out, which hardly anyone in my family had done before._
2 My father wasn't happy with my decision.
3 I knew very little about how to manage a restaurant.
4 I disagree with those who say college is useless.

> **Expressing negative ideas**
>
> There are many subtle ways to express negativity:
> Being a student is **far from / anything but** easy. (= very difficult)
> I have **hardly any / virtually no** free time. (= very little free time)
> Some subjects **aren't exactly** interesting. (= They're boring)

54

♪ Beauty school dropout, No graduation day for you. Beauty school dropout, Missed your midterms and flunked shampoo

D In groups, discuss 1–3. Do you generally agree?
1. How would your parents / friends (have) react(ed) if you('d) dropped out of college for whatever reason?
2. Do you think you have the skills to run your own business?
3. Is it better to be self-employed or to work for somebody else?

> I think it's much better to be self-employed, without a boss telling you what to do.

6 Vocabulary: Prefixes *over-*, *under-* and *inter-*

A Look at the highlighted words in the article in 5A and circle the correct answer.
1. The prefix *inter-* means ["**between" or "among**" / "**in the middle**"].
2. The prefix [**over-** / **under-**] means "too much" or "more than necessary."
3. [**Over-** / **Under-**] means "too little" or "not enough."
4. *Under-* and *over-* can be followed by [**only a verb or an adjective** / **a verb, an adjective, or a noun**].

B ▶ 5.8 Complete the call-in statements to a radio show about Victoria Sánchez. Use *under-*, *over-*, and *inter-* and the words in the box. There is one extra word. Listen to check.

| achiever (n) | act (v) | paid (adj) | perform (v) | privileged (adj) | qualified (adj) | rated (adj) | simplify (v) |

THIS WEEK'S HOT ISSUE:
Do you need a college degree to get ahead in life? What some of our callers had to say:

No, of course not!
1. "College education is ___overrated___. Intelligence and flexibility are more important. Victoria's living proof of that."
2. "I have an MBA and a PhD, but I'm having trouble finding a job. They say I'm _____. So, not very helpful!"
3. "Not having a degree doesn't necessarily mean you're going to _____ at work. Talent and the ability to _____ with people are far more important."

Yes, absolutely!
4. "We shouldn't _____ things. For some careers, like engineering and medicine, you do need a college degree."
5. "Not everyone's an _____ like Oprah Winfrey or Bill Gates. Most people need a college degree to make a decent living."
6. "A college degree is a passport to a better life. The government ought to help _____ students fund their college education, I think."

C Make it personal In groups, answer 1–4. Do you mainly agree?
1. Which statement in **B** best describes your own views?
2. If you were to start college (again) tomorrow, what would you study?
3. Do you think online courses will replace traditional teaching?
4. Do you think it's a good idea to take a year off before college?

> I've always thought taking a break after 12 years of school was a good idea, so I agree with …

Common mistake

My dad never
went to / attended
~~did/made/studied~~ college.

5.4 Did you make any mistakes yesterday?

7 Language in use

A ▶ 5.9 In pairs, imagine the story behind each photo. Listen to a radio show to check. Were you close?

The Beatles

J.K. Rowling

Walt Disney

> Well, maybe the first one is an album photo.

B ▶ 5.9 Listen again. In groups, share the additional details you understood. Then check **AS** 5.9 on p.162. Did you miss anything?

> Let's see … the Beatles got that letter in 1962.

C Do the speech balloons 1–3 mean the same as a–c below? Write S (same) or D (different).

1. I bet they wouldn't have sent that letter if they'd had a crystal ball at the time.
2. What a fighter she is. If she didn't have such willpower, she might have given up.
3. Maybe if he hadn't had so much faith in himself, we wouldn't have Mickey Mouse today!

a The executives sent the letter because they didn't have a crystal ball.
b Rowling has a lot of willpower, but she gave up.
c Mickey Mouse might exist because Disney had faith in himself.

D Which of the people mentioned would you most like to meet / have met?

> I wish I'd met Walt Disney. I bet he was a lot of fun!

E Make it personal 🌐 Search online for "famous people who weren't successful at first." Find an interesting fact to tell the class.

> I bet you didn't know this! Guess what I learned about …

♪ Why she had to go, I don't know, she wouldn't say. I said something wrong, now I long for yesterday

5.4

8 Grammar: Imaginary situations (2)

A Read the example sentences and check (✔) the correct rules.

Imaginary situations (2): mixed conditionals	
We can mix second and third conditionals:	
Situation	*Consequence*
A If Disney **hadn't kept** at it,	we **wouldn't have** Mickey Mouse today.
B If she **didn't have** such willpower,	she **might have given** up.

A = a ☐ **present** ☐ **past** situation, and its ☐ **present** ☐ **past** consequence

B = a ☐ **present** ☐ **past** situation, and its ☐ **present** ☐ **past** consequence

» Grammar expansion p.146

B ▶ 5.10 What are they saying? Complete 1–3 with the correct forms. Listen to check.

1 We _____ (be) lost now if you _____ (check) the directions.

2 I _____ (maybe join) you last week if I _____ (be) so short on money these days.

3 If I _____ (stay) in my old job, I'm sure I _____ (be) miserable right now.

C In pairs, use only the pictures to expand and role play each situation.

Common mistakes
If ~~you would have~~ *you'd* taken your phone, we ~~would have been~~ *'d be* able to call now.

9 Pronunciation: Sentence stress

A ▶ 5.11 Read about sentence stress. Listen to and repeat the sentences, slowly and then faster.

Auxiliary forms are often contracted, as in these songs, and sentence stress is on a content word.
If I'd /aɪd/ never **met** you.   You've /yuv/ lost that loving **feel**ing.
I would have /ˈwʊdəv/ **loved** you anyway.   I've /aɪv/ been **wait**ing for a girl like you.

B Make it personal Tell a story about a good or bad decision you've made.

1 Choose a topic and think about a–d.

accepting or rejecting advice   buying an expensive item   changing schools
adopting or buying a pet   getting or quitting a job   taking a trip

a When / Where / How did your decision happen?
b What happened afterwards?
c What if something different had happened?
d What have you learned from the experience?

2 In groups, share your stories. Use different conditionals and pay attention to sentence stress. Any similar experiences?

Last month I adopted a puppy. I'd always wanted to have a pet and …

5.5 How lucky are you?

10 Listening

A ▶ 5.12 Ron is telling his friend Holly about his very unlucky birthday last week. Guess what happened. Listen to the first part of the conversation and answer 1–3.

1 Where did Ron go?
2 What did Ron's boss, Barry, find out?
3 What did Barry do?

B ▶ 5.13 Listen to the complete conversation and circle the correct answers.

1 Holly [**remembered** / **forgot**] Ron's birthday.
2 Ron and Aimee are [**just friends** / **a couple**].
3 Ron and Aimee [**had** / **hadn't**] been looking forward to the show.
4 Holly [**approves** / **disapproves**] of the story Ron told Barry.
5 Ron suspects Barry was watching the show [**live** / **on a recording**].
6 Ron is [**worried** / **confident**] about Monday.

C In pairs, answer 1–3. Any differences? Has anything like this happened to you?

1 What do you think Ron's boss wants to talk about on Monday?
2 Do you think Ron's boss really saw him on TV? Is there another hypothesis?
3 If you'd been Ron, what would you have done (a) before the show and (b) when you got the text message?

> Well, maybe he just wants to catch up on Ron's work.

> Are you kidding!

11 Keep talking

A Read the quotes. How strongly do you agree? Write ++ (= strongly agree) to -- (= strongly disagree). Compare your ideas in groups. Which is the most controversial quote?

1 "Luck is what happens when preparation meets opportunity." (Seneca)
2 "Remember that sometimes not getting what you want is a wonderful stroke of luck." (Dalai Lama)
3 "Luck is believing you're lucky." (Tennessee Williams, *A Streetcar Named Desire*)
4 "I believe in a lot of things ... magic, vampires, and even ghosts, but I don't believe in luck. Good or bad." (Hillary DePiano)

> I totally agree with the first one. I mean, without hard work, luck means nothing.

> Hmm, I'm not sure. I believe some people are just born lucky.

B Make it personal In groups, tell each other about a stroke of good / bad luck you've had. Prepare using 1–5.

1 When / Where did it happen?
2 What were you doing at the time?
3 What is the main event? Why were you so (un)lucky?
4 What if something different had happened?
5 What did you learn from the experience?

> Mine is about how I came to live in Lima. I was 12 at the time and had just started high school...

♪ It ain't me, it ain't me. I ain't no fortunate one ...

5.5

12 Writing: Telling a story (2)

A Read Paul's story. In pairs, how many details can you remember?

Forum   BLOG   INBOX   MEMBERS   YOU

What's the best / worst luck you've ever had? Tell us your stories.

1 Last year, after the most stressful three years of my life, I decided that my wife and I deserved at least two weeks away from it all. Amanda was delighted with my suggestion that we go on a trip, so we took our savings and booked a five-star hotel in sunny Rio de Janeiro. If only I'd known what those two weeks had in store for me!

2 The first six days were everything we'd dreamed of. We were amazed by the beauty of the city, especially the gorgeous views. Our nightmare began on the seventh day when I got an email from our neighbor Ed saying that there had been a fire in the house! I was terrified! I wondered if I'd left the toaster on, but I thought that couldn't have caused a fire six days later! We were both devastated and, needless to say, our well-deserved vacation was ruined. Miraculously, Ed, who fortunately had our keys, managed to put the fire out. If he'd arrived five minutes later, our 80-year-old house might have burned to the ground.

3 When we got back home, we discovered that actually the fridge had started the fire – the fridge! The freezer had slowly melted, giving off awful toxic fumes. Everything was black and filthy. The insurance company was as surprised by our bad luck as we were. They had never seen anything like it before. One thing is for certain, though: We will never leave the fridge – or any household appliance – plugged in when we go away for a long break.

SHARE

B Order the events in the story 1–7.
___ There was a fire in Paul's house.
___ Paul found out about the fire.
___ Paul's neighbor put out the fire.
___ Paul wasn't sure if he'd left the toaster on.
___ Paul discovered the freezer had melted.
_1_ Paul spent six days relaxing.
___ Paul went back home.

C Read *Write it right!* Match the synonyms (1–5) to the highlighted adjectives in the story.

> **Write it right!**
> When you write a story, use a good range of adjectives, both simple (like *angry*) and more intense (like *furious*), to make your story more vivid and interesting.

1 very happy _____
2 very dirty _____
3 very upset _____
4 very surprised _____
5 very frightened _____

D Write the number of the paragraph:
The main event: ___
What was unusual about the event: ___
Background information to create suspense: ___

E **Your turn!** Write a story of 200–250 words about the best / worst luck you've ever had.

Before
Note down the main events and organize them into paragraphs.

While
Use highlighted adjectives from A to make your story vivid. Make sure the first paragraph creates suspense. Be careful with tenses, and use linking words to connect your ideas (Unit 3).

After
Record your story, and ask a classmate to listen and react. Is it what you intended?

6

Have you ever Googled yourself?

1 Vocabulary: Online privacy

A Which of the experiences shown in pictures a–e on page 61 have you had?

> Once I bought something online, and my credit card number was stolen!

B Read the article. Guess what text is missing.

PROTECTING YOUR ONLINE PRIVACY —
my two cents:

- Rule number one: Choose your passwords carefully, and stay away from obvious choices, such as your date of birth. Also, avoid using the same password across lots of different sites. Cyber criminals are everywhere these days, and _____.

- How would you feel if you were at the mall and someone followed you around with a camera, writing down every single item you looked at? That's what happens when you shop online. Even if you don't buy anything, the store is keeping an eye on you, which means _____.

- Do you have a health concern you need to talk to someone about? Or maybe a family problem you want to get off your chest? Be careful with sites containing discussion forums. _____, and this information could be accessed by future employers.

- Well, at least there's Google. Surely running a simple search is pretty safe? Well, no. _____, and your search will be kept in Google's files for months or even years.

C Extracts 1–4 are from the article. Match the highlighted words to their meanings a–d.

1. whatever you look up may appear in your search history
2. they might break into a vulnerable site and steal your password
3. they might sell all your shopping habits to third parties
4. they might keep records of every status update you post and every *like* you click on

a ☐ people not directly involved in something
b ☐ try to find a particular piece of information
c ☐ save information in order to refer to it in the future
d ☐ access illegally

D ▶ 6.1 Put the extracts back into the article. Listen to check. Think of one new way to fill in each blank.

E Make it personal In groups, discuss the concerns in the article. Do you think they pose serious dangers? Which of you is the most security-conscious online / in the real world?

> I don't understand what's wrong with the last one.

> Hmm, I don't know. What if Google remembers confidential information?

> I live in a dangerous neighborhood, so I'm always thinking about safety!

♪ Let me be the one to give you everything you want and need. Baby good love and protection. Make me your selection

6.1

a

b

c

d

e

2 Listening

A Which problems are shown in pictures a–e?

> In the first one, she's shopping, and someone could steal her personal information.

B ▶ 6.2 Listen and match five conversations about online privacy to pictures a–e.

C ▶ 6.2 Listen again. T (probably true) or F (probably false)?
1 Rob's mother-in-law likes him.
2 Jerry is Don's boss.
3 Cathy and Daniel are close friends.
4 Lynette worries about her online privacy.
5 Sophie's mother is a frequent online shopper.

D ▶ 6.3 Complete 1–5 with *risk* words. Listen to check. Then remember the sentences using only the pictures.

| risk (v)   risky (adj)   risk-free (adj) |
| at risk   at your own risk |

1 Well, OK, whatever. Play it _____.
2 I thought the whole thing was _____. How was I to know they'd use my real name?
3 I don't want to _____ losing her over a stupid Google search.
4 You know you're _____, right? I mean, using the same password.
5 Isn't online shopping a bit _____?

E Make it personal In groups, discuss 1–4. Any surprises?
1 Something you did at your own risk, despite your parents' advice.
2 Something risky you do more often than you should.
3 Three things worth risking your life for.
4 The greatest risk to the survival of humanity.

> **Common mistakes**
> Parents shouldn't listen ∧^to / eavesdrop ∧^on / spy ~~in~~^on their kids' private conversations.

> My parents wouldn't let me ride a motorcycle, but as soon as I got a job, I bought one.

> Mine wouldn't let me skateboard.

> Crazy! Not even walking is risk-free!

6.2 Do you worry about your privacy?

3 Language in use

A Read the blog. In pairs, answer 1–4 with A (Andrew) or Z (Zoë), and underline the evidence.

1. Who's afraid of past secrets hurting him / her?
2. Who called someone and demanded action?
3. Whose career is suffering because of online information?
4. Who has been confused with a relative?

The online privacy blog

HOME | **BLOG POSTS**

There are lots of reasons why you might want to de**lete** yourself from the web: embarrassing photos, opinions you no longer have, fake social media acc**ou**nts – you name it. Our readers share their stories of how they at**temp**t**ed** to disappear from the web. For**ev**er.

✉ Sept 14, 10:03 a.m.   Reply to post #1

Andrew, Chicago: A dis**t**ant re**l**ative with the same first and last name was ar**rest**ed for tax ev**a**sion a while back. He had his sentence re**duc**ed for good behavior and is now out of jail. So it all **ended** well, right? Wrong. Whenever people Google me, his arrest is the first thing **linked** with my name. I'm unemployed at the moment and, because of this **mix**-up, I have been **turned** down by three different em**ploy**ers this month, which isn't fair. I shouldn't be pe**nalized** for something I didn't do!

✉ Sept 14, 10:42 a.m.   Reply to post #2

Zoë, Calgary: About ten years ago I wrote a comment on an article in a well-known newspaper in Canada, including personal details about myself. Last year, I Googled myself and, to my ho**rr**or, saw my response in the a**r**chive section of the newspaper. Now, who knows how this information might be **used**? I **picked** up the phone and told them I **wanted** to have my profile **deleted** immediately. So far they haven't been very coo**p**erative.

Reply to Thread

B Make it personal In groups, answer 1–3.

1. Who do you feel most sorry for? Why?
2. Who do you think will have the most trouble in the future?
3. What advice would you give someone whose privacy has been invaded? Online? Offline?

If your identity is stolen, you should contact the bank immediately.

C 🔊 6.4 Read "-ed" endings. Then, in the blog, circle the /t/ or /d/ verbs and box the /ɪd/ verbs. Listen to check, echoing the verbs as you hear them.

> **"-ed" endings**
>
> Remember, "-ed" endings are pronounced either /t/ (lik**e**d, kiss**e**d, stopp**e**d) or /d/ (play**e**d, rain**e**d, call**e**d). The "-e" is silent. Only pronounce the final "-e" /ɪd/ when the verb ends in "t" (start**e**d) or "d" (need**e**d).

♪ Can call all you want but there's no one home, and you're not going to reach my telephone

6.2

4 Grammar: Using passive structures

A Study 1–3 and complete the grammar box. Then find two examples of each type of passive in the blog.

> **Using passive structures:** *be*, modal verbs, and *have*
>
> 1 **Be** + past participle: I **have been offered** a job by three different employers.
> 2 Modal verb + **be** + past participle: I **shouldn't be arrested** for something I didn't do.
> 3 **Have** + object + past participle: Tom **had his cell phone stolen**.
>
> a In 1–3, which is more important? ☐ the action ☐ who did the action
> b In 3, who stole the cell phone? ☐ Tom ☐ someone else
> c When you don't want to emphasize who did the action, you can use the ☐ active voice
>   ☐ passive voice.

» **Grammar expansion p.148**

B Rewrite the underlined items in the passive.

> **Common mistake**
> My brother is ~~been~~ *being* bullied on Facebook®.

Seven ways to say good-bye to the Internet – *forever!*

1	First, ask yourself why you're leaving the web. Just fed up, or <u>is anyone bullying you</u>?
2	Stop and think things through carefully. Remember: You <u>can't undo the steps below</u>.
3	Focus on well-known sites first, where <u>you can delete your profile</u> more easily.
4	If you've created sites on the Internet, <u>you must completely remove them</u>.
5	Check all the mailing lists you've subscribed to, and <u>have somebody remove your name</u>.
6	Check with your phone company to make sure <u>they haven't listed you online</u>.
7	Sometimes you'll need help from a real person so <u>you can have him / her erase your identity</u>.

C Make it personal Take part in a discussion about digital technology.

1 Answer A (agree), D (disagree), or NS (not sure).
 a Facebook® should be treated like a social network, not a diary.
 b You can have your "real" life ruined by too much social networking.
 c Teenagers' Internet activity must be closely monitored by their parents.
 d Digital technology is beginning to control us.

2 ▶ 6.5 Listen to three friends discussing topic a. Do they all agree?

3 ▶ 6.6 **How to say it** Complete the chart. Listen to check.

Responding to an argument	
What they said	What they meant
1 I _____ agree more.	I agree.
2 I don't _____ it that way.	I disagree.
3 OK, _____ taken.	That makes sense, I admit.
4 Look, here's the _____ .	Listen to what I'm about to say.
5 What's your _____ on it?	What do you think?

4 For two minutes, plan what you can say about topics a–d in step 1. Then in groups, compare ideas. Use *How to say it* expressions. Any disagreements?

> Facebook® shouldn't be a diary!
>
> I couldn't agree more.

6.3 What makes you suspicious?

5 Reading

A Using only the title and photo, guess what the magazine article is about.

| Home | World | Business | Sports | Health | Tech | Entertainment | | Search |

I, the Spy
by Jo O'Donnell

This isn't easy to admit, but I felt slightly embarrassed a while back when I was watching a news report about the National Security Agency's (NSA) surveillance program – the one that allowed the government to spy on its citizens, eavesdrop on phone calls, and monitor Internet traffic. Why? Because over the past decade, I have kept my children under strict surveillance in pretty much the same way: capturing instant messaging logs, eavesdropping on Skype® conversations, and even using spy software to keep tabs on what they typed. I have been the biggest threat to my children's privacy.

A few years ago, when I casually mentioned this to a friend, she was horrified. How could I do this, she asked, when it was such an invasion of my children's privacy? At the time, I made the same argument that generations of parents before me have probably made, which is that my children have no expectation of privacy while they are still living under my roof. If invading their privacy was what it took to protect them, then obviously I had every right to do so. Or did I?

The NSA once stated that what the agency did could be justified on security grounds, since it allowed the agency to identify potential terrorist threats to the U.S. So I made a similar argument to myself about monitoring my sons' online activity – after all, all I wanted was to protect them from the kinds of trouble teens get into, especially drug abuse and bad relationships. Was I right to do so? To be honest, I'm not sure. Yes and no, I suppose. Anyway, it's been quite a while since I last spied on my two sons (the youngest of whom is now turning 17), but looking back, I think I've learned some important lessons.

B Quickly read the article in two minutes to check. Does Jo …

☐ feel spying on the kids was the right thing to do? ☐ regret it? ☐ have mixed feelings about it?

C ▶ 6.7 Re-read and listen. T (true) or F (false)?
1. Jo thinks government / parental surveillance are two completely different things.
2. She told a friend it was OK to spy on the kids until they left home.
3. She used to spy on the kids mostly to keep them safe from cyberbullying.
4. She hasn't spied on the kids for some time.

D What nouns do the underlined words in the article refer to? Draw lines to them.

E ▶ 6.8 Listen to part of an interview with Jo. Number the lessons she learned 1–3. Then circle A or B.

Lessons		
☐ I learned my son had impressive talents.	☐ It's important for couples not to have secrets.	☐ None of the dangers I'd anticipated came true.
A He wrote fiction online. B He was leading an online book group.	A My husband already knew I was spying. B My husband was really upset.	A They talked about homework and school stress. B There was very little cyberbullying.

♪ I always feel like somebody's watching me. And I have no privacy

6.3

F Make it personal In groups, answer 1–4. Any surprises?
1 Do you think Jo acted appropriately? Are the lessons she learned important?
2 How much freedom do / did you have as a teenager?
3 Do you think teenagers have too much, too little, or just enough freedom these days?
4 What do you think of people who read others' texts or WhatsApp® messages? Is it ethical?

> My parents were too strict, so I'll be easier on my kids. How about you?

> I'm not sure I'll ever have kids, but I wouldn't spy on them.

6 Vocabulary: Privacy words and expressions

A ▶6.9 Listen to five short conversations between parents and their teenagers. Which two match the pictures? Do any of the people remind you of your parents?

B ▶6.10 Re-read paragraph 1 in **5A**. Match the highlighted words to their meanings. Listen to check.

1 surveillance   a ☐ keep yourself informed about something
2 spy on   b ☐ the act of watching someone who might be doing something illegal
3 eavesdrop on   c ☐ listen secretly to a private conversation
4 keep tabs on   d ☐ someone or something that is potentially dangerous
5 threat   e ☐ watch someone secretly

C In pairs, cover and remember both pictures in **A**. Then role play the conversations.

> In the first one, the woman was about 50 and she was wearing ...

> Mom, I just can't believe you were using my computer! Are you ...?

> Yes, I am. As your mother ...

D Make it personal Complete 1–4 with a word or expression from **B**. Answer Y (yes), N (no), or S (sometimes). In groups, compare ideas. After five minutes, take a vote on each question. How many unanimous opinions?

Is it OK for ...
1 employers to _____ their employees' phone conversations when they're talking?
2 parents to install _____ equipment in their children's cars and _____ their driving?
3 the government to monitor people's Internet activity to identify a potential _____?
  What do you think of people who expose government surveillance? Is it ethical?
4 couples to _____ each other's text messages and recent calls?

> Hmm ... I'm not sure. Isn't everyone entitled to a little privacy?

> I think employers have a right to eavesdrop on conversations.

6.4 Are you into social media?

7 Listening

A In pairs, answer 1–3. Any surprises?
1. Guess what the people in the photo are doing.
2. Why do some people feel the need to keep tabs on their friends?
3. Do you know any apps that make it easy for friends to spy on each other?

> All of my friends spy on me on Foursquare®, and I hate that!

Common mistake
> Facebook® lets your friends ~~to~~ see all the stuff you like.

B 🔊 6.11 Listen to James, Audra, and Tom, and match the three columns. There's one extra threat. Do you identify with any of the speakers?

Speaker	App	Privacy threats
1 James	Instagram®	teachers
2 Audra	Foursquare®	friends
3 Tom	Facebook®	boss
		family

C 🔊 6.11 Listen again. T (true) or F (false)?
1. James's parents respect his privacy on Facebook®.
2. His friends like Facebook® better than he does.
3. Audra posts photos of where she's been.
4. She has changed her privacy settings.
5. Tom uses Foursquare®.
6. He knows how to use apps correctly.

8 Pronunciation: Blended consonants

A 🔊 6.12 Listen to the rule and examples. Then complete 1–4 with the words you hear.

> Two similar consonant sounds are usually pronounced as one.
> Do you have a minu**te to** spare?
> My paren**ts s**eem totally obsessed with Facebook®.

1. It's _____ _____ ask before you take a photo.
2. _____ _____ app take a picture of you?
3. What if I _____ _____ stay home?
4. _____ _____ addictive.

B Make it personal Draw lines connecting the similar consonant sounds in these questions 1–4. Then ask and answer them.
1. Do your (grand)parents seem to value the Internet?
2. Do you see any future reasons to maintain libraries?
3. How do you think communication will change over the next 100 years?
4. How could the World Wide Web bring more peace to the world?

> My grandparents are amazing. They're really into technology.

♪ I'm free to be whatever I, whatever I choose. And I'll sing the blues if I want

6.4

9 Grammar: Question words with -ever

A ▶ 6.13 Match the phrases. Then listen to check. Check (✔) the correct rules in the grammar box.

1 He comments on whatever …
2 The answer is always the same whoever …
3 They stop and take a photo whenever …
4 However you look at this Instagram® craze, …
5 Wherever you are, …
6 Whichever app I use, …

a ☐ I always end up doing something wrong.
b ☐ you just access the app and check in.
c ☐ you talk to.
d ☐ he sees on my newsfeed.
e ☐ they see something "interesting."
f ☐ it's just pointless.

Question words with -ever: *how, who, what, which, when* and *where*

1 **Ever** means "no matter who, what, or which" in ☐ **all** ☐ **some** of the examples.
2 Question words with -*ever* ☐ **always** ☐ **sometimes** go at the beginning of the sentence.
3 ☐ **Use** ☐ **Don't use** a comma at the end of the clause when an -*ever* word begins the sentence.

» Grammar expansion p.148

B ▶ 6.14 James, Audra, and Tom continue the interview from 7B. Complete 1–5 with a question word with -*ever*. Listen to check. How would you answer the reporter's questions?

REPORTER: And what's your favorite social app?
JAMES: I love Vine®. ¹_Whenever_ I see something funny, I just video it. I mean, how cool is that? Wechat® is another favorite. I can stay in touch with my friends ²_____ I am.
REPORTER: And are there any apps you like?
AUDRA: Flickr® is OK for ³_____ likes photographs. Tumblr® isn't bad, either. I just use ⁴_____ I click on first.
REPORTER: OK. What about your favorite app?
TOM: ⁵_____ people may say about Facebook®, it's still my number one app. I love it.

C Make it personal Make 1–4 true for you. In pairs, compare. Any similar answers?

1 Whenever I hear the song (*Yesterday*), I think of (my grandpa).
2 Wherever I go, I need to tell [my girlfriend] where I am.
3 Whatever happens this year, I will try to [exercise more].
4 I totally [agree/disagree] with whoever said that [money doesn't buy happiness].

Whenever I hear the song *Summer*, I think of my ex. He used to love Calvin Harris.

Yeah, that's a great song. It reminds me of my trip to New York in 2015.

6.5 Who do you share your secrets with?

10 Listening

A In groups, answer 1–2. Any surprises?

1 Why does the interviewer in the cartoon prefer to look at candidates' Facebook® profiles?
2 How can your Facebook® page help you to get a job / stop you from being hired? Think about:

"We no longer look at résumés. We go straight to your Facebook® page."

AREAS OF CAUTION

a Pages you like

b Your choice of words

d Religion and politics

c Photos you post

e Photos you're tagged in

> The photos you post might make them think you're not serious enough for the job.

B ▶ 6.15 Listen to Larry, from the cartoon, talking to his wife about the interview. Which area of caution in **A** did he ignore?

C ▶ 6.15 Listen again and circle the right alternative.

1 The interview was [**short** / **long**].
2 They said they wanted someone [**younger** / **more experienced**].
3 Larry [**worked** / **didn't work**] at Apple®.
4 Larry [**was** / **wasn't**] late for the interview.
5 Larry's photo was taken [**indoors** / **outdoors**].
6 His wife is [**supportive** / **critical**] of him.

11 Keep talking

A In groups, what advice would you give for each area of caution in 10A? Any differences of opinion?

B **Make it personal** What advice would you give for these areas?

be happy   look your best 24/7   spend your money more wisely   impress your English teacher
make a perfect burger   stay out of trouble at college   live to be a hundred   shop online safely

1 Brainstorm as many ideas as you can.
2 Share the best ones with the class.

> I think to be happy, it's important not to worry.

> Yes, but you should be careful not to spend too much money, though!

♪ Hey, hey, you, you, I know that you like me. No way, no way. No, it's not a secret

6.5

12 Writing: A *how to ...* guide

A Read *Watch out!* Write the correct area of caution in 10A for each paragraph.

B Read the guidelines for an effective "how to ... " article. Underline examples in *Watch out!*

> 1 Create a catchy title.
> 2 Use section headings.
> 3 Write a short introduction / conclusion.
> 4 Add details.

C Read *Write it right!* Write guidelines for email etiquette (1–4).

Write it right!

When writing a "how to ..." guide, it's important to be very specific and tell the reader the dos and don'ts.

Dos	Don'ts
1 Do your best to ...	1 Avoid + noun / *-ing* verb
2 Be sure to ...	2 Whatever you do, don't ...
3 As far as possible, try to ...	3 Never, ever ...

include   reply   scan   write

1 within 24 hours – ✓ [your best]
 Do your best to reply within 24 hours.

2 huge attachments – ✗ [avoid]
 _____

3 your messages for viruses – ✓ [sure]
 _____

4 in CAPS – ✗ [whatever]
 _____

D **Your turn!** Write a "how to ... " article in about 150–180 words.

Common mistake

Try ~~to don't~~ *not to* spend money on things you don't need.

Before
Choose a topic from 11B and in pairs, brainstorm your "Top five guidelines."

While
Pay attention to the guidelines in **B**, and use at least four expressions from **C**.

After
Share your work with your classmates. What was the most popular guideline?

WATCH OUT!

Facebook® could be sabotaging your career.

Do the math: If you joined Facebook® in, say, 2010 and have posted an average of two comments every day since then, there are currently more than 4,000 comments floating around the site with the potential to ruin you reputation. Here are five things to keep in mind.

1 *Pages you like*
The pages you're a fan of say an awful lot about you. When you respond to like requests, be selective. Do your best to keep your likes as neutral as possible.

2 _____
Watch out! If you don't want to be seen doing something embarrassing, don't post it on Facebook®. Also, avoid posting inappropriate photos. And whatever you do, don't post pictures of alcoholic beverages.

3 _____
Even if you're careful when posting status updates and photos, other Facebook® users could still get you in trouble. Be sure to keep tabs on the photos you are tagged in, and have them removed if necessary.

4 _____
Never ever – ever – use foul language in a Facebook® post. Period.

5 _____
As far as possible, try to stay away from controversial topics and avoid giving polarizing opinions.

A mantra for you: "Whatever you say leaves a trace in cyberspace!" If you're afraid of being seen, you can bet your life: you probably will be!

Review 3
Units 5–6

1 Speaking

A Look at the photos on p.50.

1 Note down everything you can remember about these people, using these verbs.

> achieve   face   overcome   pursue

2 Take turns describing the person who you admire the most.

> My hero is … He / She managed to overcome …

B Make it personal Choose three question titles from Units 3 and 4 to ask a partner. Ask at least three follow-up questions for each. What did you learn about each other?

> What's your biggest life decision so far?

> Breaking up with my girlfriend. I had to face …

2 Grammar

A Rewrite the underlined sentences using the passive.

Even before the Internet, there were many security risks. Once I was in a train station, and I thought (1) <u>someone was watching me</u>. I wasn't sure, though, and I needed to make a phone call, so I took out my phone card. The phones were all in a row, and (2) <u>anyone could see them</u>, but it never occurred to me that might be a problem. Two weeks later, the phone bill arrived. (3) <u>They had charged me $1,200!</u> (4) <u>Hundreds of people had placed calls from all over the world!</u> A police officer explained that (5) <u>they had read my phone card with a pair of binoculars</u>, and (6) <u>they had captured my password</u> as I typed it, too. Even before the technology we have today, (7) <u>criminals victimized many people.</u>

B Make it personal In pairs, use the words below to tell a story about yourself or someone you know. Use at least six passive sentences.

> capture   eavesdrop on   post   remove   see   spy on   tag   watch

> I knew someone who was spied on as he was …

3 Self-test

Correct the two mistakes in each sentence. Check your answers in Units 5 and 6. What's your score, 1–20?

1 I'm sick of my mom listening my conversations and my dad spying my friends.
2 Jenny has been turn down for the first job, but she been interviewed for another.
3 I had stolen my computer by some thieves, and however I looked, I couldn't find it.
4 It's important to achieve a career and solve any obstacles.
5 My dad face a lot of setbacks, but after he moved to the U.S., he find work immediately.
6 I wish I would speak English better – if only I learn those verb tenses!
7 My job isn't precisely easy, and I have hardly no free time.
8 My mom wasn't able to do college, and it bothers her not to have studies.
9 If I hadn't keep at it, I wouldn't have been so successful now.
10 She's an underachiever, but if she didn't have determination, she wouldn't have win the race.

4 Reading

A Read the title. In pairs, what do you think the article might be about? How many ideas can you think of?

Your Facebook® password and you

You might find this incredibly hard to believe, but more and more employers are asking job candidates for their Facebook® passwords. Get ready. It could happen to you on your next interview. But do you have to agree? Absolutely not! Protect yourself. Never, ever give your Facebook® password, under any circumstances, to a potential or current employer.

Why not? You might think if you're a discreet person and haven't posted anything risky. Be aware. You could still find yourself in legal trouble. First of all, your friends, who have posted on your timeline or written you what they thought were private messages, have not granted permission. They may sue you and your company for invasion of privacy if they find out a company is reading their correspondence. They also haven't given permission for your company to see their photos. And just imagine what might happen if one of your friends applies for a job at the same company and is turned down. You could be in big trouble if your friend suspects discrimination.

And what if you're the employer? You may think your right to information is protected, but you may be wrong. You could be accessing sensitive personal information that would be illegal to ask for in an interview. And again, your candidate's friends have not given you permission for third-party access. Even if you escape legal action, is what you're doing ethical? You wouldn't ask to read through your candidate's personal mail before making a job offer – or would you?

B In pairs, note down reasons not to give your employer your Facebook® password. How many can you remember?

C Fill in the missing words in these actions that may be illegal and write A (Applicant) or E (Employer). Did any of them surprise you?
1 Letting an employer read _____ messages from friends.
2 Allowing an employer to see _____ taken of friends.
3 Allowing access to information if your friend applies for a job and suspects _____ .
4 Gaining access to sensitive information that you could not ask for during an _____ .
5 Not having been given _____ -party access by a candidate's friends.

5 Point of view

Choose a topic. Then support your opinion in 100–150 words, and record your answer. Ask a partner for feedback. How can you be more convincing?
a You think people who overcome illness are more inspiring than those who overcome poverty. OR
You think people who overcome poverty are more inspiring than those who overcome illness.
b You think protecting your online privacy is very important. OR
You're not too worried about online privacy because you have nothing to hide.
c You think college is essential for success. OR
You think college is one option, but there are many other ways to suceed.

Grammar expansion

1 stop, remember, forget, and try `do after 1.2`

I **stopped to buy** some meat for dinner. (= I stopped at the store in order to buy meat.)
I **stopped buying** meat when I became a vegetarian. (= I no longer buy meat.)
I **remembered to call** Dad on his birthday. (= I didn't forget to call Dad.)
I'm sure I talked to Dad last week, but I don't even **remember calling** him. (= I don't have a memory of the fact that I called Dad.)
I sometimes **forget to call** my parents to say I'll be late. (= I don't always remember to call my parents.)
I'll **never forget calling** my parents to say I was getting married. They were so thrilled! (= I remember clearly calling my parents.)
I'm **trying to concentrate**. Please be quiet. (= I'm attempting to concentrate.)
I **tried writing** down new words, but I still couldn't remember them. (= I experimented with writing down new words.)

More on *try* and *forget*

Only use *try* + *-ing* when the meaning is "to experiment with something." When the meaning is "to attempt," use an infinitive:
I've been **trying to be** nicer to my little sister.

Only use *forget* + *-ing* to remember the past. Otherwise, use the infinitive.
I sometimes **forget to set** the alarm, and then I'm late for school.

2 Using the infinitive with adjectives: More on negative sentences `do after 1.4`

Pay close attention to the position of the negative. Whether it goes with the verb or the adjective often depends on what's being emphasized.
It's important for you **not** to go. (= You shouldn't go.)   It's **not** important for you to go. (= You don't have to go.)
It's critical for my daughter **not** to fail her exam. (= She must pass.)   It's **not** critical for my daughter to pass her exam. (= It's OK if she fails.)
Sometimes if you move the negative, the sentence no longer makes sense. When in doubt, say the sentence aloud.
It's essential **not** to feel intimidated during an interview. (= Relax and don't feel intimidated.)
~~It's **not** essential to feel intimidated during an interview~~. (= Meaning is unclear.)
Sometimes both choices are possible and have a very similar meaning.
It's **not** helpful to …   It's helpful **not** to …   pressure your children. (= You shouldn't pressure them.)

Unit 1

1A Complete 1–8 with the infinitive or *-ing* form of the verbs.
1. I remember _____ (meet) Tim at a party last year. He was thinner then.
2. We stopped _____ (look) at the flowers. They were really beautiful.
3. I'm trying _____ (finish) as fast as I can! Be patient.
4. She stopped _____ (go) to dance class. She said it was really boring.
5. At the last minute, we remembered _____ (take) an umbrella. It's a good thing because it started pouring!
6. He forgot _____ (check) that the door was locked, and a robber walked in.
7. I tried _____ (take) French classes, but in the end, I realized I liked English better.
8. I just can't forget _____ (see) Tom again after all these years. I think I'm still in love!

1B **Make it personal** Write and share three facts about yourself. Use *remember, stop, try,* or *forget*.

2A Match the sentence beginnings with the most logical ending.
1. It's important not to   a ☐ agree with everything your teenager says.
2. It's not important to   b ☐ contradict your children in front of their friends. It could embarrass them.

3. It's not essential for you to   a ☐ understand your children at all times.
4. It's essential for you not to   b ☐ have rigid opinions.

5. It's not critical for older parents to   a ☐ be stuck in the past.
6. It's critical for older parents not to   b ☐ be up-to-date with technology.

2B Choose two sentences you agree with from A. Then give a reason for your opinion.

2C Circle the most logical options. When both seem possible, circle both.

> ¹[**It's important not to / It's not important to**] think all teenagers are alike. People mature at different rates, and ²[**it's useful not to / it's not useful to**] make comparisons. If you want to have a good relationship with your teen, ³[**it's essential not to / it's not essential to**] make unrealistic demands. In addition, things were very different when you were young, and it's ⁴[**critical not to / not critical to**] be close-minded. Teens listen to their friends more than their parents, and it's ⁵[**helpful not to / not helpful to**] begin sentences with "When I was your age … "

> **Bonus! Language in song**
>
> ♪ It's been a hard day's night, and I've been working like a dog.
>
> - What do you think the expression "a hard day's night" means?
> - Give the singer from 1.3 on page 11 some advice beginning with "It's important (not) to …"

Grammar expansion

1 Sentences with complements and conjunctions do after 2.2

Sentences with complements can be followed by a conjunction and another sentence.			
Less formal	The most difficult thing about having children is it's expensive,	**and**	it's hard work, too.
	The advantage of working is I make money,	**so**	I'm looking for a job.
	The great thing about exercise is losing weight,	**but**	it's time-consuming.
More formal	The problem with teenagers is they don't think.	**Furthermore,**	they don't listen.
	The problem with English is pronunciation.	**Therefore,**	I need more practice.
	The great thing about technology is being connected all the time.	**However,**	it's expensive.

Common mistake

The problem with coffee is it keeps me ~~up so~~ *up, so* I never drink it at night.

The great thing about coffee is the ~~taste, however,~~ *taste. However,* it keeps me up.

2 More on modals do after 2.4

Using modals in negative sentences		
	Present	Past
Maybe it's true.	There **might / may not** be aliens.	It **might / may not** have visited us.
I'm pretty sure it's true.	It **must not** be a ghost.	You **must not** have seen him.
I really doubt it's true.	You **can't / couldn't** be serious!	It **can't / couldn't** have been an alien.

Common mistake

He ~~mustn't~~ *must not* have been home. He would have opened the door. I'm pretty sure.

Mustn't expresses prohibition in British English (American English = *can't*), but it cannot express probability.

Using modals in continuous sentences		
	Present	Past
Maybe it's true.	They **might / may (not) be watching** TV.	He **might / may (not) have been** robbing the house.
I'm pretty sure it's true.	It **must (not) be raining**.	You **must (not) have been paying attention**.
I really doubt it's true.	You **can't / couldn't be thinking** clearly!	We **can't / couldn't have been driving** that fast.

Common mistake

He ~~must have been~~ *was probably* being influenced by others.

Modal verbs are not used in the passive in continuous tenses.

1A Combine two advantages of fast food, or an advantage and a disadvantage, to give five opinions with conjunctions. Watch your punctuation!

Advantages	Disadvantages
it's ready made	it's not fresh
it tastes good	it usually has too much salt
it doesn't go bad	you don't know how old it is
it's not expensive	it's bad for you
you always enjoy your meal	children need healthy food
children love it	
they sell it everywhere	

The good thing about fast food is that it's ready made. However, you don't know how old it is.

1B Share in pairs. How many different combinations did you make in A?

2A Rewrite the underlined parts of the sentences with an affirmative or negative modal verb.
1. <u>I really doubt there's</u> life on other planets. We would have had some visitors by now.
2. I'm worried about Tim. He didn't answer his phone, but <u>maybe he was sleeping</u>.
3. <u>I'm pretty sure Sheila didn't take</u> her keys, and that's why she had to sleep in a hotel.
4. <u>I'm pretty sure Amy wasn't paying attention.</u> That's why she had an accident.
5. <u>I really doubt a monkey was climbing</u> in the window! You must have seen a shadow.
6. Roger didn't show up for his appointment because <u>I'm pretty sure he didn't remember it</u>.

2B Complete the story with past modal verbs in the continuous form, using the verbs in parentheses.

Ape costume or the real thing?

No one would believe this, but a gorilla ¹*might have been living* (maybe / live) in my neighborhood last year. It was filmed on video at about 1:00 a.m. one Saturday night. At that moment, a car ²_____ (probably / approach) because the headlights revealed a gorilla's face on a video the neighbors had installed to monitor coyotes. Then, suddenly, it disappeared.

It ³_____ (maybe / hide) behind some parked cars because no one could find it. I think the gorilla was frightened. It ⁴_____ (probably / not / expect) to see anyone.

When I told the story to my brother, though, he said the neighborhood ⁵_____ (probably / imagine) things. A gorilla ⁶_____ (very much doubt / walk) in the neighborhood. A person ⁷_____ (probably / wear) an ape costume. He or she ⁸_____ (maybe / come) home from a party.

2C Make it personal Using modals, share something surprising about your own neighborhood that you can't explain.

> I think someone might be living on our roof. I found a shoe in the elevator!

Bonus! Language in song

♪ All day long I think of things, but nothing seems to satisfy. Think I'll lose my mind if I don't find something to pacify.

Rewrite this song lyric from 2.1, beginning with "The most difficult thing about my day is ... " Then combine the two sentences in the song with a conjunction.

Grammar expansion

1 Uses of the past perfect (do after 3.2)

The past perfect is used to avoid misunderstanding.	
When my boyfriend **got** home,	he **texted** me. (= the actions occurred almost simultaneously)
	he **had already texted** me. (= he texted before he got home)
By the time my boyfriend got home,	he **had (already) texted** me. (= identical in meaning to above)

1 Always use the past perfect with *by the time*. Add *already* to avoid ambiguity.
2 We often avoid the past perfect when a misunderstanding is unlikely, even if one action clearly takes place before another.
▶ I **didn't get up** in time to have breakfast before I left for school.
▶ When the singer **walked** on stage, everyone **applauded.**

Common mistake

Oh hi, I ~~hadn't seen~~ *didn't see* you earlier. Sorry I didn't say "hello."

The past perfect is common with these expressions:
I was already working **by the time** I'd started college.
I didn't start studying English **until after** I'd finished high school.
I had studied English **before / previously**, but I didn't remember much.
I had **already** bought a house when I got married.
I hadn't bought a house **yet** when I had children.
I **still** hadn't saved much money when I turned 30.
Up until last year, I'd never met anyone from the U.S.

2 Past narration (do after 3.4)

Use *used to* and *would* to set the scene. Then use past tenses to show the order of events and whether they were continuous.

We **used to live** in an old house, and every so often we **would hear** noises. One day, I **was brushing** my teeth when I **heard** a strange, high-pitched sound. Before I could figure out where it **was coming** from, I **saw** glass on the floor. Someone or something **had broken** the window.

Unit 3

1A Complete the conversations with the correct form of the verbs in parentheses.

1. A: When I was a child, I really _____ (enjoy) playing alone.
   B: Really? I never did.

2. A: When I arrived at the party, everyone _____ (leave).
   B: You mean no one was there at all?

3. A: When Susanna arrived at the airport, her brother _____ (greet) her warmly.
   B: I bet she was really happy to see him.

4. A: Hello, when I _____ (call) this morning for an appointment, no one _____ (answer) the phone.
   B: Oh, we're so sorry. When would you like to come?

5. A: When Amy met George, she _____ (already / date) several other guys.
   B: Yes, but he was "the one" for her from the second she saw him!

6. A: I was so worried about Tim when he disappeared on our hike.
   B: Yes, when Sue and I finally saw him, we _____ (run) up and _____ (hug) him.

1B Make it personal Complete 1–6 so they are true for you. Use each verb only once. Share with a partner. Did you learn anything new?

> be decide do go learn start

1. Up until last year, I _____ .
2. I _____ yet when I _____ .
3. Before I _____ , I _____ never _____ .
4. Until after _____ , I _____ .
5. By the time I _____ , I _____ already _____ .
6. I still _____ when I _____ .

2A Circle the correct forms to complete the story.

> I ¹[**used to love** / **would love**] going to the beach, and I would go there whenever we could. One day I ²[**was** / **had been**] in the car with some friends when all of a sudden, I ³[**realized** / **had realized**] I had left my bathing suit at home. By the time I ⁴[**discovered** / **had discovered**] I didn't have it, we ⁵[**drove** / **had driven**] for over three hours. I still ⁶[**didn't go** / **hadn't gone**] swimming that summer, so I decided to make a bathing suit. First, I ⁷[**took** / **had taken**] my blouse, and I cut off the sleeves. Then I ⁸[**rolled** / **had rolled**] up the bottom and tied it to look like a bikini. I ⁹[**saw** / **had seen**] a friend do that previously, and it looked like a real bathing suit. Then I ¹⁰[**did** / **had done**] the same with my jeans. And here's the selfie I ¹¹[**took** / **had taken**]! Only after I ¹²[**went** / **had gone**] swimming and everyone had complimented me on my new bathing suit, did I realize that I ¹³[**had** / **'d had**] no clothes to wear home!

2B Make it personal When was the last time you left something important at home? Complete the paragraph. Who has the best story?

> One day I _____ when I realized I'd forgotten my _____ . By the time I remembered, I _____ . When I arrived at _____ , I had to _____ . To this day, I still _____ .

> **Bonus! Language in song**
>
> ♪ I **used to rule** the world, Seas **would rise** when I **gave** the word, Now in the morning I sleep alone, Sweep the streets I **used to own**.
>
> Which verbs in **bold** can be replaced by a different past form?

143

Grammar expansion

1 Using conjunctions (do after 4.2)

Common conjunctions fall into several categories of meaning.		
Adding	Comparing / Contrasting	Conceding
besides	unlike	although
moreover	while	even though
what's more	whereas	though
	but	despite
	however	in spite of

Some can be followed by more parts of speech than others. Notice the position of *not* in negative statements.		
Although Even though While	my phone's **not** expensive, (sentence)	it works great.
Despite In spite of	the fact that it's **not** expensive, (clause) **not** being expensive, (*-ing* form)	it has tons of features.
	the expense, (noun)	I buy a new phone every year.

2 More on reflexive pronouns (do after 4.4)

Some verbs are commonly used with reflexive pronouns.
Be careful! You'll **cut yourself**. Melanie dived into the pool and **hurt herself**. I really **enjoyed myself** last night at the party. I met Sam at the concert when he came up and **introduced himself**. Can you believe John and Louise **taught themselves** to speak Arabic?
Other verbs: *prepare, dry, help, imagine, express*

Other verbs, however, only use a reflexive pronoun for emphasis.
I forgot to **shave** today. I hope it's not obvious! I forgot to **shave myself**. I was in a really big hurry this morning.
Other verbs: *feel, shower, get dressed, get up*

And some verbs, such as *concentrate* or *focus*, don't use reflexive pronouns.
I couldn't **concentrate** in class today. I was so tired!

Unit 4

1A Combine 1–7 in two different ways, using the conjunctions in parentheses.

1. I did a lot of research. I was taken in by the phone company's offer. (*despite* + -ing; *although*)
   Despite doing a lot of research, I was taken in by the phone company's offer.
   Although I did a lot of research, I was taken in by the phone company's offer.
2. I still failed my English test. I studied all night. (*in spite of* + clause; *even though*)
3. I'm able to work at my own pace. I'm not a fan of the flipped classroom. (*in spite of* + -ing; *although*)
4. My friends don't make much money. They still have nicer clothes than I do. (*despite* + clause; *while*)
5. Mountain climbing can be dangerous. I really enjoy it. (*despite* + noun; *while*)
6. I read lots of hotel reviews before I went to Berlin. I still paid too much. (*in spite of* + clause; *though*)
7. My brother is a genius. He's a nice person. (*besides* + -ing; *what's more*)

1B Make it personal Changing only the second part of the sentence in A, share four facts about yourself. Any surprises?

> Although I did a lot of research, I still bought the wrong computer.

1C Find and correct Amanda's four mistakes. Then role play the conversation ending with "No, none at all!"

JIM: Your English has really improved in the last year.
AMANDA: You really think so? Despite study every day, grammar is still difficult.
JIM: But you have a really good accent.
AMANDA: Well, in spite of I might have a good accent, I still have a long way to go.
JIM: Maybe you could practice grammar by having a language exchange: you know, find someone who wants to learn Portuguese.
AMANDA: That's a good idea. I really try. However that my English will never be perfect. Conjunctions are so difficult!
JIM: Well, you just have to feel comfortable.
AMANDA: Yes, you're right. In spite of it's challenging, I should keep at it.
JIM: Yes, that's it.
AMANDA: How's my grammar today? Did I make any mistakes?
JIM: Well, just a few small ones!

2A Circle the correct options to complete the paragraph about Sayeed's visit to New York.

Every night I dreamed about my vacation. In my dream, I was staying ¹[**myself** / **ø**] in an expensive hotel, right off Fifth Avenue with my cousin Laura. Every morning we got up ²[**ourselves** / **ø**] early to sightsee. Wherever we went, we dressed ³[**ourselves** / **ø**] fashionably. In fancy restaurants, I would often introduce ⁴[**myself** / **ø**] to famous actors. We taught ⁵[**ourselves** / **ø**] to think like celebrities, and in general, we felt great ⁶[**ourselves** / **ø**]! But, of course, it was all a dream, and at 7:00 every morning, I had to wake up ⁷[**myself** / **ø**], shower ⁸[**myself** / **ø**], and go to work.

2B Correct the mistakes.

1. I'm having trouble focusing myself in class. I'm always tired.
2. The students looked at them in the mirror and were pleasantly surprised by their appearance.
3. I went to a concert last night, and I really enjoyed.
4. When my daughter concentrates herself, she can succeed at anything.
5. My grandparents were immigrants, but they taught himself to speak perfect English.

Bonus! Language in song

♪ It took myself by surprise I must say. When I found out yesterday. Don't you know that I heard itself through the grapevine?

Are the reflexive pronouns correct? Correct the mistakes.

Grammar expansion

1 Imaginary situations: *hope*, *wish*, *if only*, and *supposing* `do after 5.2`

Future	I **hope you'll be** quiet during the performance. (= I don't know if you'll be quiet.)
Present	I **wish you'd be** quiet when I'm talking. (= You're not quiet, and it's annoying me.)
Past	I **hope** I **didn't fail** my test. (= I don't know if I failed.)
Past	I **wish** I **hadn't failed** my test. (= I failed, and I'm sorry I did.)
Future	**If only** I **could see** Sarah again. (= I don't think I'll ever see her again and I miss her so much.)
Past	**If only** I **could have seen** Sarah again. (= I didn't see her and I'm sure we would have gotten back together.)
Future	**Supposing** Sarah **wanted** to go out with you again, would you say yes? (= It's unlikely Sarah will want to go out with you again.)
Past	**Supposing** Sarah **had wanted** to go out with you again, would you have said yes? (= She didn't want to go out with you again.)

Common mistake

I ~~wish~~ *hope* I'll be able to go out tonight.

2 Shortening conditional sentences `do after 5.4`

Zero, first, second, third, and mixed conditionals can all be shortened when the information referred to is understood. The auxiliary cannot be contracted.

Zero	My brother never **helps** me. If / When he **does** (help me),	I feel better.
First	I don't think my sister **is coming**. If she **is** (coming),	I'll be really happy.
Second	I **don't have** my parents' help. If I **did** (have my parents' help),	I'd go to college.
Third	I **didn't have** my parents' help. If I **had** (had my parents' help),	I would have gone to college.
Mixed	We **didn't make** any money. If we **had** (made money),	we wouldn't be living here any longer.

All conditionals can be contracted in a shorter way also.

| First | **With** my parents' help, I'll be able to go to college. |
| Third | **Without** my parents' help, I wouldn't have gone to college. |

1A Complete the sentences with the correct form of *hope* or *wish* and the verb.
1. A: I _____ Ann _____ (call) me tomorrow. I really need to talk to her!
   B: Oh, I'm sure she will.
2. A: I _____ my mother _____ (spend) more time with me when I was young.
   B: I feel the same way. Mine was always working.
3. A: I really _____ I _____ (not fail) my final exams.
   B: I'm sure you'll do well if you study!
4. A: I _____ I _____ (know) how to drive. It's such a useful skill.
   B: Why don't you take lessons?
5. A: John _____ he _____ (not quit) school.
   B: Yes, that wasn't too smart. You need a college education these days.
6. A: I _____ I _____ (not upset) my little brother when I yelled at him.
   B: I don't think he's upset. Look, he's smiling!

1B Which is the full form? Write *had* or *would*.
1. Sue wishes she**'d** apologized sooner. *had*
2. Jim wishes I**'d** asked him to the party.
3. I wish they**'d** hurry up and finish.
4. We all wish they**'d** come to visit last year.
5. I wish they**'d** decide about this year.
6. I wish you**'d** sent the package yesterday.

1C Make it personal Share three hopes and three wishes that are true for you.

> I really hope I ... , and I really wish I ...

2A Rewrite these short sentences using the word *if*.
1. With hard work, you can learn anything.
   If you work hard, you can learn anything.
2. Without good grades, I never would have gotten into college.
3. With really good luck, maybe I'll win the lottery.
4. Without studying really hard, I wouldn't have passed the exam.
5. Without a lot of practice, you'll never learn to speak English.
6. Without the help of my parents, I wouldn't be living in this house today.

2B Shorten the underlined parts of each sentences, beginning with the word in parentheses.

When I was young, I didn't have many role models. ¹<u>If I'd had good role models</u> (with), I wouldn't have ended up in so much trouble. ²<u>If I hadn't had the support of my neighbor Melanie</u> (without), I'd still be on the streets. She convinced me that I should go back to school. ³<u>If I didn't go back to school</u> (if), she said, I'd be tempted to live a life of crime. ⁴<u>But if I had a good education</u> (with), I'd have a satisfying career. I really listened to her. ⁵<u>If I hadn't listened to her</u> (if), I might still be running around with those guys. I'll always be grateful to Melanie. ⁶<u>If I didn't have her</u> (without), who knows where I'd be today.

2C Make it personal Write three sentences about your own role model. Be sure to use short conditional sentences. Choose from these topics or one of your own.

Someone who helped you ...
make friends   stay out of trouble   choose a career
understand your parents   learn a new skill
meet your boyfriend / girlfriend

I'll always remember the boy who sat next to me at my new school. Without him ...

Bonus! Language in song

♪ *I can be your hero, baby, I can kiss away the pain.*

Rewrite this song line beginning with *I hope*, *I wish*, or *If only*.

Grammar expansion

1 Questions in the passive `do after 6.2`

		Subject	be	Verb (+ by)
Simple present	Are	you	–	(ever) watched by your parents?
Present continuous	Are	you	being	bullied online?
Simple past	Were	you	–	(ever) spied on as a child?
Present perfect	Has	your profile	(ever) been	broken into?
Future	Will	teachers	be	replaced by computers?

The pattern is the same with question words.

How often	has	your profile	been	accessed?

Causative sentences are always passive in meaning. The causative with *get* is a little more informal.

	Auxiliary	Subject	*have* or *get*	Object	Verb (+ *by*)
Present continuous	Are	you	having / getting	your hair	cut by Ralph?
Simple past	Did	Amy	have / get	her sentence	reduced?

Using the passive

The passive is very common in English and makes impersonal questions sound polite.
Can the phone **be exchanged** after 30 days?
Could I **have** my hard drive **checked**, please?

Common mistake

How many people ~~were~~ *was* your profile seen by?

Be careful with subject-verb agreement!

2 Uses of *whatever* `do after 6.2`

In spoken English, *whatever* often expresses strong advice or a warning:
▶ **Whatever** you do, don't talk about politics on Facebook®.

Whatever is also used to end conversations and avoid arguments:
▶ "You spend far too long online!" "Yeah, yeah, **whatever** (you say)."

Fixed expressions like *whatever that means* and *whatever it's called* can be used when you don't know, remember, or understand something:
▶ Mom says she's going to keep tabs on me "selectively," **whatever** that means.

1A Put the words in order to make questions. (Each has one extra word.)
1. to / by / ever / will / replaced / paper books / be / e-books / ?
2. does / why / still / is / considered / the iPad / a revolution in teaching / ?
3. being / students' / should / from the classroom / banned / be / native languages / ?
4. removed / be / from / always / photos / have / Facebook® / you / when friends ask you to / ?
5. privacy / can / your / be / how / you / violated by credit card companies / ?

1B Make it personal Ask and answer the questions. How many similar opinions?

1C Make conversations 1–4 more natural and polite. Replace the underlined sentences with sentences in the passive.
1. A: <u>I'd like you to check my computer, please.</u>
   B: OK, right this way.
2. A: <u>Should you replace the battery?</u>
   B: Yes, that would be a good idea.
3. A: <u>Will you repair this water damage by tomorrow?</u>
   B: We'll certainly try our best.
4. A: <u>Have you fixed my phone yet?</u>
   B: We're very busy today, ma'am. I promise we'll get to it.

1D Trivia time! Complete 1–5 with questions in the passive. Then search on "fun trivia" and create two more questions.

1. Where _____ ?
   The Soccer World Cup? I think it was held in Brazil in 2014, wasn't it?
2. How many _____ ?
   The song *Imagine*? I'm sure it's been recorded well over 100 times. And translated, too!
3. Who _____ ?
   Everyone knows that! The Sistine Chapel was painted by Michelangelo.
4. Where _____ ?
   Ceviche? That's that dish with raw fish and citrus juices, isn't it? I think it's eaten throughout Latin America.
5. Where in the world _____ ?
   It's obvious you haven't been to Paris. The Mona Lisa can be seen at the Louvre!

2A Replace the underlined phrases with these expressions. There is one extra.

> whatever you do   whatever the cost   whatever time   whatever   whatever that means

1. A: Oh no, why isn't the site loading?
   B: It says here "bad gateway," <u>but I'm not sure what that is</u>. Let's try Bruno's iPad.
2. A: So you're moving on Sunday?
   B: Yeah, and <u>even if it's really expensive</u>, I've decided to use a moving company.
3. A: But you said you wanted to go to the concert!
   B: <u>It doesn't matter</u>. I've changed my mind.
4. A: I'm taking my first trip abroad next month.
   B: Great, but don't let your credit cards out of your sight, <u>under any circumstances</u>.

2B Make it personal Start a conversation about home, school or leisure. How many ideas can you think of?

... and I mean it!

Yeah, yeah, whatever! That's the third time you've said the same thing in the last ten minutes.

Bonus! Language in song

♪ I always feel like somebody's watching me. And I have no privacy.

Make the first sentence in this song line passive.

Selected audio scripts

▶ R1.1 page 26 exercise 1

A = Amy, J = Joe

A: Did you grow up around here?
J: Well, no, we moved here when I was 16 so I could start over.
A: What do you mean?
J: You know how teenagers do some stupid things. They say our minds aren't fully developed until we're 25. I had some problems – peer pressure, that sort of thing.
A: And you had to leave town?
J: Well, that's one way to look at it. My friends weren't the best influence. The biggest problem was that they convinced me to take risks. Need I say more?
A: Oh! I guess not …
J: And so my grandparents decided it was time to leave.
A: Your grandparents? Did they live with you?
J: Yes, I was raised by them. They were great. My grandfather was a movie actor, and my grandmother a novelist.
A: Wow! That must have been cool!
J: And how about you? What was your childhood like?
A: Well, I …

▶ 3.3 page 29 exercises 2B and C

M = Marco, L = Lucas, A = Ana

M: But that wasn't the worst part.
L: It wasn't?
M: No. It had been a stressful day, lots of tests, lots of traffic, the treadmill … and I wanted to relax before going back home, so I decided to catch a movie that night.
L: On your own?
M: Yeah. For a change, you know. I got there ten minutes before the movie started, got myself a soft drink, walked into the theater, sat down, and closed my eyes, as I waited for the lights to dim. I didn't even remember the name of the movie, you know … I just wanted to relax for a while.
L: Uh huh.
M: A bit. So, anyway, I sit down, and I glance across the room, and I see someone who looks familiar. I mean, really familiar.
L: Uh huh.
M: But the theater was really dark, so I couldn't get a good look at her. Well, the lights go out, the movie starts, and the next thing I know the woman moves three rows back and sits right in front of me.
A: OK, go on.
M: I couldn't take my eyes off her … I kept staring at her and, bingo, it was my sister-in-law – or at least that's what I thought.
A: That's what you thought?
L: Oh no!
M: I wanted to say hi … So, I whispered something in her ear and gave her hair a little pull, you know. I was sure she'd be happy to see me there.
L: Oh boy. Here it comes.
A: You pulled the woman's hair?
M: Very, very lightly, just to get her attention.
L: And then what?
M: You wouldn't believe what happens next.

▶ 3.4 page 29 exercise 2D

L: And then what?
M: You wouldn't believe what happens next. The woman's hair comes off.
L: What? She was wearing a wig?
M: Yeah. It was totally false.
A: Oh, boy!
M: So she turns around and screams and …
L: Oh no!
M: Before I know it, everybody's staring at us, telling us to be quiet, and …
A: So what happens next?
M: I don't know. I just apologized, got up, and ran to the exit.
L: Oh, man.
M: I've never been so embarrassed in my entire life.

▶ 3.11 page 33 exercises 6C and D

S = Sue, A = Ann

S: So, Ann … How did you two meet?
A: Well, I was doing a college assignment. It was nearly midnight, and I was **sick and tired** of studying. So I took a break and took the dog for a walk.
S: That late?
A: Yeah! Every **now and then** I do that. Anyway, then I saw this guy walking his dog, and he looked really familiar. Turns out it was Vince, an old boyfriend from high school! I'd seen him on Facebook®, but I never thought we'd meet **face to face** again after all these years.
S: Wow! Did he recognize you?
A: Yeah. We met for coffee the very next day. Then time went by, and we started seeing each other nearly every day. Before we knew it, we were madly in love.
S: You seem very happy!
A: I am. Well, naturally, there have been problems along the way, and we've had our **ups and downs**. But we're crazy about each other, and I want him in my life for **better or worse**.
S: Wait a second! Are you talking marriage?
A: Sure. Maybe this year, maybe next year, maybe five years from now. But it's going to happen **sooner or later**. It's written in the stars.
S: Wow! To think how it all started … Talk about serendipity!
A: Ser-en-dipity, yeah, love it! Definitely my favorite word in the English language.

▶ 5.9 page 56 exercise 7A

DJ = DJ, K = Keith, L = Lorna

DJ: Welcome back to *Oops, wrong again*, your weekly radio show about unusual careers. Keith, your story reminded me of the Beatles back in 1962.
K: You mean when they got rejected by Decca records?
DJ: Exactly. Apparently Decca's executives wrote to them saying that guitar groups were on the way out, or something like that. Can you believe it?
K: I bet they wouldn't have sent that letter if they'd had a crystal ball at the time. The best-selling band in history!
L: Oops! But at least they signed the Rolling Stones soon afterwards. And what about J.K. Rowling? She got rejected by twelve different publishers.
K: Twelve?
L: Yeah. They thought the book was far too long for kids.
DJ: So what happened in the end?
L: Well, she found a publisher whose president gave it to his eight-year-old daughter. Guess what? She loved it. So they agreed to publish Harry Potter.
K: I really look up to Rowling. What a fighter she is. If she didn't have that kind of willpower, she might have given up …
DJ: That's so true, … and she wouldn't be one of the wealthiest women in the world today.
K: Oops! Walt Disney had his ups and downs, too. He was fired from his job as a newspaper editor, wasn't he?
L: He sure was! In 1919. They said he lacked imagination and had no good ideas. Maybe if he hadn't had so much faith in himself, we wouldn't have Mickey Mouse today!
DJ: And that would be a real shame … That sure is swell! See ya soon!

iDentities

WORKBOOK

1.1 What's the story behind your name?

A Answer Amir's riddles about members of his family.

1. I have a cousin, Sam. Sam's wife's mother is Sam's _____.
2. Zubeida, my lovely _____, is my husband's child from his first marriage.
3. My _____ is 101! He's my dad's granddad.
4. I don't have any (half) brothers or sisters, so that makes me an _____.
5. My sister and I are _____. I call her my little sister though, because she's two minutes younger than me!
6. My father's grandfather's great grandson is my _____.

B Complete the missing family words in Suzie's blog.

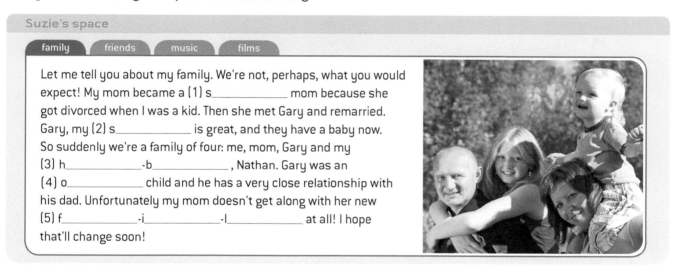

Suzie's space

family | friends | music | films

Let me tell you about my family. We're not, perhaps, what you would expect! My mom became a (1) s_____ mom because she got divorced when I was a kid. Then she met Gary and remarried. Gary, my (2) s_____ is great, and they have a baby now. So suddenly we're a family of four: me, mom, Gary and my (3) h_____-b_____, Nathan. Gary was an (4) o_____ child and he has a very close relationship with his dad. Unfortunately my mom doesn't get along with her new (5) f_____-i_____-l_____ at all! I hope that'll change soon!

C ▶1 Use five of these verbs in the correct form to complete conversations 1–5. Listen to check.

| bring up | get along | look after | look up | make up | run in |

1. A: Is your family very competitive?
   B: We sure are, especially my brother and me. We had a huge argument over a basketball game last weekend, but we _____ again afterwards!
2. A: Athletic success _____ your family, doesn't it?
   B: Yeah, especially on my dad's side. He was a professional skier. My grandma was a professional skier, too. And now I'm one.
3. A: Does everyone _____ well in your family?
   B: Yes, well, except for my two grandfathers. They don't like each other at all!
4. A: Is there anyone that you really _____ to in your family?
   B: Yes, my grandma. She had eight kids! Can you imagine that? She was amazing.
5. A: How often do you have to _____ your younger brother and sister?
   B: Not often. They're both in their teens now so they don't need adult supervision in the evening.

D Write true answers to two of A's questions in **C**.

1. _____
2. _____

1.2 Do / Did you get along with your parents?

A Read the online forum. Check (✓) the problems you had (or have) with your parents.

B Replace the bold *get* verbs with these verbs in the correct form. One is used twice.

> arrive at   become   have an opportunity
> receive   understand

Q What annoys you about your parents?

When I'm in the bathroom for ten minutes or more, they **get** angry and start banging on the door.
1 _____

My parents are always criticizing my look. It's like, why are you wearing jeans and that T-shirt? They just don't **get** me.
2 _____

I never **get** to watch what I want on TV. My dad's always in the living room, watching sports programs.
3 _____

If I don't **get to** the table in time for meals, they start calling me on my phone. "Where are you?" It drives me crazy.
4 _____

When I was a kid, all my friends **got** an allowance, but did I? No! Never. I had to wash the car or look after my baby brother just to get $5.
5 _____

My mom **gets** really mad when I don't clean my room. But I don't see why. After all it's mine, not hers!
6 _____

C Order the words in 1–6 to make sentences.

1 asking / not / help / bad / idea / is / for / a
_____

2 on / but / we / started / carried / tennis / raining / playing / it
_____

3 it's / to / on / not / going / exhibit / Sunday / the / worth
_____

4 baby / new / a / having / exhausting / is / totally
_____

5 help / about / nervous / next week's / can't / feeling / I / exams
_____

6 ideas / new / thinking / for / a / of / hard / time / have / I / work
_____

D Make it personal Rewrite two sentences in **B** so they're true for you.

1 _____
2 _____
3 _____

How many pets have you lived with? 1.3

A Read the blog post and check (✓) its main purpose.
1 To offer advice for pet owners.
2 To make people laugh.
3 To complain about the author's pet.

B Re-read and match underlined phrases 1–3 with definitions a–e. There are two extra ones.

a ☐ a lot   b ☑ ever   c ☐ mostly
d ☐ in reality   e ☐ anywhere

IS YOUR CAT PLOTTING TO KILL YOU?

Don't get me wrong. I love pets. I wouldn't hurt an animal ¹ <u>in a million years</u>. The thing is, would they say the same about us? When your kitty is lying in front of the radiator in a state of complete happiness, is she dreaming of being a tiger in the jungle, hunting wildlife … or hunting you?

How to tell if your cat is plotting to kill you? is the subject of a book and an online feed, and it is the funniest site ² <u>on earth</u>. Owners take pictures of their pet when it clearly has murder in mind. Notice that look of annoyance on your cat's face? Oh yes, watch out!

The book is extremely funny, and I've started looking at my cat, Cloud, with new eyes. If she's plotting to kill me, what would she do if my hamster escaped in the living room? Cloud would be ³ <u>a thousand times</u> more dangerous to a little orange thing like that. One false move and my hamster would quickly see its Facebook® status change from "pet" to "snack." I'm starting to think that perhaps it's only our size that keeps us alive.

C ▶2 Complete what these pet owners said with a form of the word in CAPITALS. Listen to check.
1 Pet _____ownership_____ isn't easy, but it's a wonderful experience. OWNER
2 I love cats because they're so _____. AFFECTION
3 I think almost everyone in this _____ has a dog. NEIGHBOR
4 We didn't know anything about keeping a pet iguana, but the salesperson at the pet shop was very _____ and explained everything to us. HELP
5 The countryside is the best place to have a horse because you have the _____ to ride wherever you want. FREE
6 Ricky taught his parrot to speak, and now it's incredibly _____. It doesn't shut up! TALK
7 We've lost the tortoise! It's Cathy's fault. She's always so _____. This time, she left it alone in the garden, and now it's disappeared! CARE
8 Having a dog has brought us so much _____. I can't imagine life without our furry friend. HAPPY

D **Make it personal** Complete this sentence so it's true for you.
In my opinion, _____ make perfect pets because _____
_____.

1.4 What difficult people do you know?

A ▶3 Listen and number Ki-Yeon's problems in the order you hear them, 1–4. One problem isn't mentioned.

Ki-Yeon's …
- ☐ aunt is calling him a lot.
- ☐ cousin can't come to the wedding.
- ☐ family doesn't want to pay for the wedding.
- ☐ fiancée can't find a wedding dress.
- ☐ brother hasn't taken care of the invitations yet.

B ▶3 Listen again. T (true) or F (false)?
1. In Korea, it's traditional to give wooden ducks as a wedding present.
2. Ki-Yeon doesn't like his mother-in-law.
3. In Korea, the grandparents pay half the cost of the wedding.
4. The wedding ceremony is in February.
5. Ki-Yeon's cousin is expecting a baby.
6. Ki-Yeon talked to his aunt about the food for the wedding.

C Complete the wedding advice using the words in parentheses.

What are your tips for organizing a wedding?

1. _It's essential for you to tell_ everyone what time the ceremony begins. (essential / you / tell)

2. _____ your guests the details over the phone. (better / not / give)

3. _____ each guest a map of how to get to the wedding. (advisable / send)

4. _____ stressed, but you should try not to panic. (hard / not / get)

5. _____ all your guests to respond to the wedding invitations. (good / idea / you / ask)

6. _____ the food before you know exactly how many people are coming. (no / point / choose)

D Make it personal What's your best piece of advice for a close friend who's getting married next week?

_____
_____

Do you still make voice calls? 1.5

Writing an effective paragraph

A Complete the paragraph with these connectors.

> besides   it's important   lastly
> on top of that   to begin with

Smart phones: a curse for all generations?

Many parents give their kids a smartphone as a form of babysitter, even during family meals. However, (1) _____ for parents to think carefully before allowing their children to bring a smartphone to the dinner table. (2) _____ , this suggests that it's fine for children to use their gadgets on social occasions. (3) _____ , it prevents shy children from learning how to interact with other family members and makes it difficult for older relatives to begin a conversation with them. (4) _____ , many games on these devices are incredibly addictive, and children play them too much already. (5) _____ , dinner is a moment for a family to enjoy quality time together. Smartphones disrupt that happy atmosphere.

> HONEY, COULD YOU TEXT THE KIDS AND TELL THEM THAT DINNER IS READY?

B Choose the best topic sentence (a–c) to complete three paragraphs from other student essays.

(1) ☐ Teenagers are so glued to their smartphones that they lose interest in talking to other family members. Sometimes they are so engaged with the screen that they don't even say hello to their parents when they get home from work.

a Teenagers spend too much time playing games online.
b Some parents are unable to communicate clearly with their kids.
c Using technology makes teenagers antisocial.

(2) ☐ People can receive work emails or messages at the dinner table, in the bathroom, or even as they are getting ready for bed. This can increase stress levels at home when they should be trying to relax.

a The biggest problem is the number of instant messages that people send and get about unimportant things.
b It is no use thinking that someone's job stops when he or she leaves the office.
c People spend too long on the computer in the office.

(3) ☐ Children and younger teens often stay glued to their devices late into the night. This makes them tired and even angry the next day, and that causes arguments. Some educators suggest that it is essential for parents to turn the house WiFi off at night. But is that a solution? Children can still access the Internet on their phones.

a Many problems come from not getting enough sleep.
b Parents are worried about the cost of all this technology.
c The problems are worse in the evening than the morning.

C Write a new topic sentence for a paragraph in **B**, using your own ideas.

_____
_____

D Look back at lessons 1.1–1.5 in the Student's Book. Find the connection between the song lines and the content of each lesson.

E ▶ 4 Listen to the five question titles from the unit, and record your answers to them. If possible, compare recordings with a classmate.

2 » 2.1 What's most on your mind right now?

A Do the crossword. Read the clues and make noun modifiers.

ACROSS
1. I flew from London to Japan last week. The nine-hour time difference really messed up my body _____.
4. The main social _____ in our country are poverty, unemployment, and homelessness.
5. Dad was in a car _____. Another car hit him on the highway but luckily, no one was hurt.
6. The adolescent _____ is different from the adult one, so teenagers think differently from older people.
7. The patient was suffering from stress, which disturbed her sleep _____. She kept waking up in the middle of the night.

DOWN
2. Finding _____ activities you like is the best way to deal with stress. I do Zumba, a mix of dance and aerobics from Colombia.
3. We always have a big family _____ at lunchtime on Sundays, cooked by my oldest sister.
4. I find it hard to make an _____ decision. I need time to think before I say "yes" or "no".
7. _____ pressure is one of the biggest problems in high school. You feel like you have to do the same things as your friends.

B Complete 1–5 with one word each from box A and box B. Each box has one extra word.

A	family financial material physical romantic scientific

B	appearance dynamics fact possessions problems relationships

1. Someone who finds it difficult to talk to people and make friends may have difficulty in forming _____.
2. _____ occur when you spend more than you earn on a regular basis.
3. Many philosophers feel that _____ such as cars, homes, and expensive clothes are not important for true happiness.
4. _____ should not be a factor in whether a job applicant gets a job or not. It is your skills that are important, not how you look.
5. A _____ is something that is clearly true and cannot be disputed by other experts. It isn't an opinion or a theory.

C Correct the mistake in each sentence.
1. I keep worry about my flight next week. What if it gets canceled? _____
2. I think to my grandma night and day. She's been in the hospital for months. _____
3. I can't seem making any progress with my college project. It's impossible. _____
4. I can't stop to think about my operation next week. I don't want to have it! _____
5. I consider leaving my job because I'm so unhappy at my company. _____

D **Make it personal** Rewrite two sentences in **C** so they're true for you.
1. _____
2. _____

Do you worry about your diet? 2.2

A Read the interview. Replace the bold words with these phrases. There are two extras.

> a big deal   at a disadvantage   wears off
> keep you going   treat   a waste of time
> wears off   weight gain   in an accident with

Ask the expert

Miranda Blanco, triathlete

What should triathletes eat and drink?

Not sugar! Sugar gives you a big energy boost, but it soon **disappears**. If you eat lots of sugar, it may also explain **a sudden increase in kilos**. If you want chocolate or candy, eat it as a **special favor to yourself**, not a main part of your diet.

Water doesn't give you energy, but if you get dehydrated your performance will suffer. When competing in sports events, remember to drink lots of water or you'll be **in a worse position** to the other athletes.

Getting enough iron is **very important** in maintaining a healthy diet, especially for women. Good sources of iron are cereals and green vegetables like spinach.

Pasta is the super food for any athlete, especially whole wheat pasta. This releases energy slowly, so it will **give you energy** throughout your event.

1 _____
2 _____
3 _____
4 _____
5 _____
6 _____

B ▶5 Complete Miranda's comments 1–5 with one word in each blank. Listen to check.
1 The problem _____ going on a diet is that you always feel hungry.
2 The best _____ about the swimming pool is the sauna. It's the perfect place to relax.
3 One disadvantage _____ running is that it can damage your knees if you do it over a long period.
4 The good thing about _____ rice before exercise is that it gives you lots of energy.
5 The worst thing about training for the competition _____ getting up early in the morning.

C Read the article and circle the correct alternatives.

The pros and cons of eating fruit, fruit, and nothing but fruit!

In the world of weird diets, fruitarianism is the most extreme of all. Fruitarians only eat fruit, no vegetables, and nothing cooked. The best thing about the diet is ¹*that / what* people discover exotic fruit from around the world, like durian (pictured). The ²*worse / worst* thing about the diet is ³*can place / it can place* people in the hospital.

The biggest disadvantage of fruitarianism is ⁴*this / that* the diet doesn't include essential food groups like fat or protein. ⁵*This is / These are* necessary for a healthy body. Another disadvantage ⁶*of / to* the diet is that fruitarians don't drink coffee or eat chocolate, which ⁷*is / are* both extremely hard to give up.

Nevertheless, people can and do choose the fruitarian route. The easiest part of ⁸*be / being* a fruitarian is the first few days when the body feels different – but this is only a temporary change.

The hardest part is ⁹*keep / keeping* the diet up. That should come as no surprise. The problem ¹⁰*about / with* fruitarianism is that our bodies are not designed for a fruit-only diet, which means that there are serious health risks for its followers. It is not a long-term option for good health.

2.3 Who's the most intelligent person you know?

A Which do you think is more important in life: being intelligent or looking intelligent? Read the article to check if the author shares your opinion.

How to look more intelligent in 6 easy steps

Jervis Jameson

There is lots of advice out there on how to be more intelligent, but the truth of the matter is that appearance is more important than reality. It's better just to look more intelligent ... and anyone's capable ¹_____ looking like Einstein, without making any special effort.

1 Dress the part. When shown a photo of a woman in smart clothes and the same woman in casual wear, most people thought the first woman was more intelligent than the second one. It's amazing, but if you wear a suit to work like me, people assume you are good ²_____ your job.

2 A double negative makes a positive, e.g. "I don't dislike your work." People find it difficult ³_____ follow double negatives, and they think people who use them are more clever than others.

3 According to psychologists, people think that if someone looks them in the eye during conversation, they assume the person is highly intelligent.

4 Researchers at the University of Melbourne believe they have found a link between intelligence and people who wear glasses. It seems that eyeglass wearers really are more adept ⁴_____ doing complicated tasks. Now if I could just find mine in the mornings ...

5 It's all in the voice. If you're skilled ⁵_____ speaking slowly and clearly, people will believe you know what you are talking about. Talking loudly is a big no-no.

6 Never tell people you're intelligent. If you have a gift ⁶_____ something like math or programming, keep it under your hat. Really smart people tend to be modest in their everyday lives.

B Complete the phrases 1–6 in the article.

C Re-read and check (✓) the statements we can infer about the author.
1 Jervis Jameson believes that people can train themselves to be more intelligent. ☐
2 He's a very lazy person. ☐
3 He often wears very formal clothes. ☐
4 He's extremely serious. ☐
5 He's quite forgetful. ☐
6 He talks very loudly in his everyday life. ☐

D Complete 1–6 with a reference word.
1 I asked two people in the store to help me. The first ignored me, and the _____ refused to help me because she was on her break!
2 You can tell what kind of photo you have by _____ filename: .gif or .jpeg, for example.
3 In college, I discovered the theory of multiple intelligences, _____ completely changed how I judge the success of my students.
4 Not one student had brought a pen with _____ . They were so unprepared for my lessons!
5 There are so many people that I follow on Twitter®, but there's only _____ that always makes me laugh.
6 Harry was the person _____ intelligence test put him in the top 2% of people in the country.

Do you enjoy science fiction? 2.4

A ▶6 Listen to a discussion about the *chupacabra* ('the goat-sucker'). Who thinks it might exist (✓)? Who doesn't believe it exists (✗)?

Frank Mortimer ☐   Rachel Schultz ☐   Alba Lopez ☐

B ▶6 Listen again. Correct the wrong information in 1–4.

1 It all began in March 1995 in Puerto Rico. A farmer discovered eight goats with all their blood missing. _____

2 Eyewitnesses say that the chupacabra is gray with brown eyes. It moves like a kangaroo, and it has spines on its back. _____

3 There have been reports of chupacabras in Puerto Rico, the continental United States, Argentina, and Chile. _____

4 The coyote might have been ill. When they're ill, coyotes can become tired and gray, like descriptions of the chupacabra. _____

C Circle the correct alternatives in the comments on the *Science Fiction or Science Fact?* website.

Science Fiction or Science Fact?

1 The farmer *must / can't* have seen something strange on that night in 1995.

2 People invent stories like this all the time because they *might just want / just have wanted* to get their photo in the paper.

3 It can't *be / have been* a monster that killed those eight animals on that night. It's science fiction!

4 An animal like the chupacabra *may exist / have existed* somewhere in Puerto Rico. They're discovering new species all the time.

D ▶7 Complete 1–5 with the correct form of the verbs. Listen to check.

1 A: Pete didn't reply to my email yesterday.
   B: He might not _____ (see) it.

2 A: I saw Kim over the weekend, but I didn't have time to speak to her.
   B: What? It can't _____ (be) Kim. She was in Chicago!

3 A: Jim's lost his coat. He can't find it anywhere.
   B: He may _____ (leave) it in the cafeteria. He had it when we ate lunch.

4 A: Look at this. The bank says I have $2,000 in my account, but I didn't put it there.
   B: Someone at the bank must _____ (make) a mistake.

5 A: Did it rain last night? The laundry isn't dry.
   B: It couldn't _____ (rain). Look, the ground isn't wet.

2.5 What was the last test you took?

A for-and-against essay

A Complete the essay with these connectors.

> a further advantage   a number of drawbacks   one advantage of
> on the one hand   on the other hand   to sum up   ~~while~~

Modern students are being tested to death. Discuss.

Teachers and parents are worried that students are taking too many tests. Some students take a test after every unit of their coursebook ¹_____while_____ others have frequent exams throughout the year.

²_____ frequent tests is that they show what students really know. Today all the knowledge in the world is one click away. In a test, students must show clear understanding of their subject. ³_____ is that tests motivate students to study.

However, there are ⁴_____ to frequent testing. Tests take up a lot of class time that could normally be better spent teaching. Tests are also demotivating for weaker students. Furthermore, the purpose of these tests is not always clear, for example, just to give teachers a quiet class. ⁵_____, tests are an opportunity to spot which students are struggling and to see where review is necessary.

⁶_____, these tests might actually be simply to prove that schools are teaching the approved syllabus set by the government. In other words, the tests may not actually be for the benefit of the individual students at all.

⁷_____, students are taking too many tests, and these are occupying class time that could be better used in other ways. Tests should only be given when there is a clear need for them, for example, as a final exam. Other forms of evaluation can be much fairer and more productive.

B Decide if 1–4 are F (for) or A (against) the title "Modern students are being tested to death."

1 Tests for ten-year-olds may only be a simple test of their ability, whereas many ten-year-olds feel under enormous pressure to pass them.

2 One further drawback is that the more tests there are, the less time there is for fluency practice in language classes, as it is not practical to give speaking tests to 40 or more students each week.

3 Although it can be argued that students take too many tests today, schools in my country actually tested students more in the past than they do today.

4 One further advantage of testing is that it prevents cheating. Students cannot simply cut and paste an answer that they have "Googled".

C Write your own conclusion to the for-and-against essay question in **A**.

To sum up, _____

_____.

D Look back at lessons 2.1–2.5 in the Student's Book. Find the connection between the song lines and the content of each lesson.

E ▶8 Listen to the five question titles from the unit, and record your answers to them. If possible, compare recordings with a classmate.

3.1 Do you get embarrassed easily?

A Do the verb puzzle. Then choose the correct picture a–d for 8 (the word in gray).

1 To open your mouth, usually wide, because you're tired, sometimes with a rude noise!
2 To open a door by moving it away from you.
3 To fall because you accidentally hit something with your foot.
4 To look at something for a long time without looking away. It rhymes with *hair*, *pear*, and *square*.
5 The opposite of clue 2. It rhymes with *full* and *wool*.
6 To look at something quickly for a short time, then look away. It rhymes with *dance*.
7 To express emotion or pain with a long, loud, high sound. It rhymes with *seem* and *dream*.

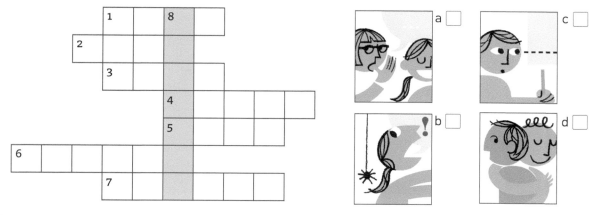

B Cross out the incorrect choice for each sentence.

1 The official *glanced / pushed / stared* at my passport photo when I arrived at the airport.
2 A lady *screamed / whispered / yawned* my name, but I'd never seen her before.
3 A tall man *glanced / tripped / pushed* me when I was trying to get on the bus.
4 We *pushed / pulled / screamed* the dog out of the car.
5 The lion *stared / whispered / yawned* while I took its photo.

C ▶9 Complete the conversation with these words. There's one extra. Listen to check.

| believe | but | happens | go | know | then | thing |

A: Did I tell you about my work trip last week?
B: No, ¹_____ on. Continue.
A: Three colleagues and I are traveling to a conference with our boss. He's going to drive, so he tells us to meet him in the parking lot. But when we get there, it's full of cars, and we aren't sure where he is.
B: So what ²_____ next?
A: I call him and I say "We're in the parking lot next to this really old red car that looks like a maniac has been driving it". Before I ³_____ it, everyone's staring at me.
B: And ⁴_____ what?
A: I just keep talking. I say, "Yeah, yeah, the car has these bumps and scratches and a really stupid 'Dog on board' sign in the back window." You won't ⁵_____ what happens next. My boss says "That's my car."
B: Oh no!
A: The next ⁶_____ I know, the car door opens and my boss gets out. He looks absolutely furious. He doesn't talk to me all the way to the meeting – and it's a four-hour trip! I just wanted to die!

3.2 How often do you take selfies?

A Read the article and circle the correct alternatives.

"There are selfies and there are selfies"

Japanese astronaut Aki Hoshide ¹*traveled / was traveling* on the International Space Station when he ²*took / had taken* the selfie of the year. Hoshide ³*had worked / was working* outside the Space Station when he ⁴*captured / had captured* his perfect snap.

If you look carefully in his helmet, you will see what made this photo so special. Hoshide ⁵*had waited / had been waiting* second after second for the perfect moment when the earth and the space station both ⁶*appeared / had appeared* in a straight line. In the instant when the earth ⁷*arrived / was arriving* at the right spot, Hoshide ⁸*hit / had been hitting* the button. After he ⁹ *was putting / had put* the picture on the Internet, Twitter ¹⁰*went / had gone* crazy. There are already almost 3,000 retweets of the selfie from space. Beat that, Ellen DeGeneres!

B ▶10 Complete 1–6 with the correct form of the verbs. Listen to check.

1 I took an amazing selfie while I _____ (walk) around Washington D.C. In it, you can see me standing on Pennsylvania Avenue, with a great view of the White House behind me. Gorgeous!
2 I was on a boat and I was about to take a photo of a whale when I _____ (drop) my camera in the water! And it would have been the best picture ever! What a shame!
3 It was only when I looked at my camera and saw some terrible photos that I realized my six-year-old son _____ (take) photos with it.
4 My favorite childhood photo was taken when my parents, my brother, and I _____ (camp) in the woods. The expression on my face shows how happy I was.
5 We saw Novak Djokovic, the tennis player, but I couldn't take a photo because I _____ (leave) my camera at home.
6 Someone took a photo of me while I _____ (watch) a baseball game, and it ended up in the newspaper!

C Make it personal What's the best selfie you've ever taken? Use 1–3 from **B** as a model to help you.

_____

_____

What invention can't you live without? 3.3

A Read the blog below about hot new inventions and check (✓) the correct options in the chart.

	The author likes it	The author doesn't like it	The author gives no opinion
1 Ice cream			
2 Toasting knife			
3 PEG			

B From the context, guess the meaning of the bold words in the blog. Match them to definitions 1–8.
1 cut into thin parts, as we do with meat, cheese, or pizza _____
2 people who don't eat any animal products _____
3 an expression meaning *something is my responsibility* _____
4 expensive _____
5 a long thin object that can be metal or wood – nature, it's part of a tree _____
6 useful _____
7 appears when you don't expect it _____
8 visible when there's no light _____

Innovations round-up
Katerina Oblov

Summer's here, and we're all feeling a little bit lazy over at HQ. Nevertheless, now and again a fun new gadget still **pops up** on our Facebook page. **It's up to me** to let you know what's out there. Here are July's top-three innovations:

1 We've just discovered something that is completely different – **glow-in-the-dark** ice cream. It comes in several different flavors, including raspberry, and its light comes from a natural food flavoring. Not being made with any dairy products, it's suitable for **vegans** and people who cannot drink milk.

2 The handheld toasting knife is out of this world. I've never seen anything like it before. The knife heats up and toasts bread while you **slice** it. It makes perfect toast time after time. It's my pick of the month.

3 In our office, we've been arguing a lot about PEGs (personal energy generators). Basically, a PEG is a **stick** that you carry, and while you move, walk, or run it generates energy. You then use it as an emergency battery. Basically, people who are into adventure sports like hiking think it's really **handy**. Sooner or later the battery always runs out though, usually when you're miles and miles away from anywhere. I'm more of an indoor person and I'm not eager to buy the PEG that I saw, especially because at $200 each, it's pretty **pricey**.

C Complete 1–6 with binomials.
1 My parents have been married for fifty years. They've had their ups and _____ like any couple, but they still love each other enormously.
2 What do you think are the pros and _____ of taking early retirement?
3 Diana put her heart and _____ into writing that book, so she was so disappointed when it never got published.
4 I'm afraid this is the apartment we've rented, so for better or _____, we're now stuck with it.
5 I was walking along a beach in Cancún when I suddenly came face to _____ with my boss!
6 We've told him over and _____ not to forget to recharge his laptop, but he never listens!

3.4 What was your favorite activity as a child?

A ▶11 Listen to a conversation about childhood fads. Complete 1–6 with *Ron* or *Mary*.
1 _____ got into the fad at the age of 12.
2 _____ always used to eat the same thing while doing the activity.
3 _____ used to do the fad in the 1980s.
4 _____ started the fad after receiving a birthday present.
5 _____ stopped the fad while still at school.
6 _____ wants to do the fad again in the future.

B ▶11 Listen again. T (true) or F (false)?
1 Ron used to dress up in special clothes when playing role-playing games.
2 Ron used to play the games in the dining room.
3 Ron plays the games with his children.
4 Mary used to go roller-blading with her friends and her family.
5 Mary's roller-blades were lots of different colors.
6 Mary doesn't have any roller-blades now.

C Correct the mistake in each extract.
1 When I was twelve, my mom used to buy me a surfboard. We lived next to the beach, and I would go surfing every weekend. _____
2 I used to play basketball every week. We used to win the State Championship once in 2009. _____
3 When I was a kid, I would to collect comics. I would go to the local comic-book shop once a week, and I'd buy loads of different ones. _____
4 I wasn't use to have any hobbies when I was a kid. The educational system in my country was very strict, and we used to have a lot of extra classes in the evenings. _____

D Make it personal Complete the sentences so they're true for you.
1 As a child, I used to _____ after school, and then I would _____ or _____ .
2 A few years ago, I didn't use to _____ , but now I do it all the time.
3 When I was a bit younger, I used to _____ a lot, and once I _____ .

What makes you really happy? 3.5

Telling a story (1)

A ▶12 Read the story and circle the correct alternatives. Listen to check.

Last month I was at my college library because I wanted to use the computers. I put my flash drive into the machine ¹*as / initially* I logged on and waited. ²*Eventually / Initially*, nothing happened, so I waited, but the PC wouldn't recognize my flash drive. ³*All of a sudden / Some time later*, I decided to restart the computer. It took ages to restart so ⁴*finally / in the meantime*, I started sending some WhatsApp® messages on my smartphone. As I was tapping on my phone, the girl next to me was looking at me angrily. I didn't know why so I ignored her. ⁵*Eventually / At first*, the computer started up again, but it still wouldn't recognize my flash drive. I was starting to get really annoyed because it still wasn't working, so I put the flash drive in and out again several times. ⁶*All of a sudden / As*, the girl next to me leaned over, looking like she wanted to speak to me. ⁷*Finally / In the meantime* she said, "Could you please stop trying to put your flash drive into my computer!"

B Replace the bold words in each sentence with a synonym.

1 I nervously opened the letter from the government. **At first**, I thought I owed money, but in the end, I realized that they were actually paying me. Yeah! _____
2 The water went off **just as** I was having a shower. My hair was full of shampoo, and we didn't have any more water for the rest of the day! _____
3 I made the sandwiches for our son's party. **Meanwhile**, my wife made the cake. _____
4 I tried calling the office for hours, but nobody replied. **In the end**, I realized that it was five o'clock in the morning in their country! _____
5 We were having coffee when **all of a sudden** Billy screamed. There was a huge spider under the table! _____
6 I was chatting with this guy because I thought he was a new student in our class. **Some time later**, I discovered that he was our new teacher! _____

C Correct the mistake in each extract.

1 I was walking down the street in L.A. last month when all of a suddenly, I saw Jennifer Lawrence! _____
2 I put this video online and forgot about it. Well, some time late, I discovered that it had gone viral in Canada. It was amazing. _____
3 Jim did the ironing. In the meanwhile, I cleaned the bathroom. _____
4 I almost had an accident on my bike. I was riding down the street, and there was a tree in the road. I didn't see initially it, but luckily, I stopped in time. _____
5 We spent ages trying to buy tickets for the concert online, but after while, we just gave up. It was impossible. _____

D Look back at lessons 3.1–3.5 in the Student's Book. Find the connection between the song lines and the content of each lesson.

E ▶13 Listen to the five question titles from the unit, and record your answers to them. If possible, compare recordings with a classmate.

4 » 4.1 Are you ever deceived by ads?

A Read the story and circle the correct alternatives.

Spider in ear is a web of lies

You've all seen the video. A man has a pain in his ear. He goes into the bathroom. He can't figure ¹*out / over* what is causing his discomfort until he reaches over the sink and – gross! – discovers that a spider is living in his ear.

All the online media outlets were completely taken ²*in / off* and ran the story along with the video. Unfortunately, it turned ³*in / out* to be a hoax!

So how come all these journalists and editors fell ⁴*for / off* the trick once again? It's because this was not a video made by a teenager in his bedroom, but the work of Bruce Branit, a special effects professional.

Branit knew what people watch ⁵*away / out* for when they try to spot a fake. Great images and special effects often give ⁶*away / over* the fact that the video is a fake. Instead, Branit used a simple iPhone® and made the image shaky, so it looked amateur. Only an expert can tell a fake and a real video ⁷*off / apart*.

The image of the spider in the ear may seem unbelievable … because that's exactly what it is!

B ▶14 Put the words in italics in order to complete the conversation. Listen to check.

A: Look at this video! It shows an eagle attacking a man in a park.
B: Come on! *that / surely / agree / you'll* ¹_____ it's a fake.
A: It's on a real news website.
B: Just because it's on a newspaper's website *mean / authentic / it's / doesn't* ²_____ .
A: I tell you it must be real. *way / it / look / at / this* ³_____ . How could they train an eagle to do that?
B: *point / missing / the / you're* ⁴_____ ! None of this is real. There is no eagle. They can make a bird using special effects. A kid can do that on a computer.
A: You're just a cynic.
B: *me / way / another / it / let / put* ⁵_____ . How could they be filming at the exact moment when the eagle attacked? It's almost impossible.
A: That's why it went viral – because it's a unique video!
B: Honestly, you'll believe anything. You should go and work for one of those websites.

C Make it personal Complete the sentences so they're true for you.

1 The last online video I fell for was _____ .

2 What gives me away when I get embarrassed is _____ .

3 The last time I bought something that turned out to be a complete waste of money was _____ .

Are teachers important in the digital age? 4.2

A Read the blog about Keele University in the U.K. True (T) or False (F)?
1. All courses at Keele are taught face to face.
2. The blog author found the equipment difficult to use at first.
3. KAVE prepares students better than traditional teaching methods.

B Complete the blog with these conjunctions.

| despite | even though | in spite | unlike | whereas |

The anatomy of the classroom of the future

¹_____ I had chosen to study Anatomy, I was still feeling nervous when I began my course at Keele University in the UK. ²_____ my friends who were studying history and languages, I was on an intense, challenging science course. They were studying books, ³_____ I was studying the human body.

So I was delighted on my first day to discover KAVE (the Keele Active Virtual Environment). It's a virtual reality program for students like me.

To use KAVE, I was given special glasses and a special stick, which was used to zoom in and out on things I was seeing. ⁴_____ of the fact that it was my first time in a virtual classroom like this, I soon got the hang of it, and I became absorbed in my work. I used it to travel around a hospital as if I were a doctor.

It is amazingly realistic. The system has been a great success for almost everyone who has tried it. ⁵_____ not having the same amount of physical contact with patients and illness, students who used KAVE consistently got better grades at the end of the course. It is the classroom of the future, today!

C Match 1–5 to a–f to make sentences. There is one extra ending.
1. Schools today have interactive whiteboards unlike
2. Although my teacher is not a native speaker of English,
3. In spite of practicing it for hours with my teacher,
4. We learned a lot of English in school despite
5. TV programs in Spain are usually dubbed into Spanish

a ☐ I still can't pronounce the rolled 'r' in Spanish!
b ☐ while those in Turkey are in the original language with subtitles.
c ☐ mine, which had a blackboard and a piece of chalk!
d ☐ to have no coursebooks at all.
e ☐ the fact that we had classes with 50 students!
f ☐ she's one of the best I have ever had.

D **Make it personal** Complete the sentences so they're true for you.
1. Even though I've been learning English for quite a while, _____.
2. Despite having read a lot in English _____.
3. Unlike listening in my own language, listening in English _____.
4. In spite of my accent in English, _____.

4.3 What was the last rumor you heard?

A Read and complete the urban legend with questions a–f. There's one extra.
- a Where does this urban legend come from?
- b How did criminals find out about it?
- c Why did the banks never introduce this system?
- d What is the ATM hoax?
- e Are there any other problematic PINs?
- f What happens when you do that?

Urban legend of the week: the ATM Hoax

This week, we're talking to Sally Redmond about one of the most famous tricks of recent times, the ATM hoax.

Q: ¹ _____

Back in the day, people said that if someone tried to steal money from you at an ATM, you should enter your PIN number backwards.

Q: ² _____

It's like an instruction. This tells the bank that someone is trying to rob you. It sounds an alarm, and the police should arrive **in no time**.

Q: ³ _____

It all started in a 1980s news article that discussed this idea as a suggestion from a bank. In fact, the suggestion was never adopted, so the news article is out-of-date. And today? **At first** someone must have come across the original story and written about it on Facebook. Then it went viral through Twitter. And it re-appears **from time to time**.

Q: ⁴ _____

It doesn't work. **In the end**, they abandoned the idea because they realized that lots of people have a PIN that reads the same backwards and forwards, like 2552.

Q: ⁵ _____

How about one like 1131? **At some point**, a user is going to hit the wrong key and enter 1311 by mistake. Are the police going to come running every time that happens? This whole story is just an urban legend, nothing more.

B Replace the underlined words with the bold phrases in **A**.
1. I tried to dissolve a tooth in soda when one fell out. <u>After a long time</u>, nothing happened. _____
2. They told me that Taylor Swift was going to play a secret gig in my city. <u>In the beginning</u>, I believed them, but I soon realized it was just a rumor. _____
3. <u>A long time ago</u>, people said that if you ate carrots, it improved your eyesight – and actually it's true. They contain vitamin A, which is essential for good vision. _____
4. If you talk about the moon landing, <u>there will always be a moment when</u> someone will say it's a hoax and it never happened. Get real, people! _____
5. <u>Occasionally</u> you read these stories in the paper about someone finding a frog or an insect in a bag of salad in the supermarket. They gross me out! _____
6. You often hear stories about people finding something horrible in a burger in the fast-food restaurant, and <u>almost immediately</u> it's all over the Internet. It's hard to tell if these stories are true or false. _____

C ▶15 Complete 1–6 with these phrases. Listen to check.

| a bird | a broken record | cats and dogs | a glove | wildfire | the wind |

1. **A:** The doctors struggle to control this disease.
   B: I know. It's unstoppable. It spreads like _____ .
2. **A:** You didn't really get along with your sister, did you?
   B: Not at all. We fought like _____ when we were little.
3. **A:** Your horse is fast, isn't she?
   B: You're telling me! She runs like _____ .
4. **A:** This bus is always full of people! I hate it!
   B: You say that every time we get on it. Honestly, you sound like _____ .
5. **A:** How was the dress? Did you try it on?
   B: It's like it was made for me. It fits like _____ .
6. **A:** Kaitlin is looking really thin these days. I'm really worried about her.
   B: Yes, she does a lot of exercise, but she eats like _____ .

How would you describe yourself? 4.4

A ▶16 Listen to the podcast on look-alikes: people who look the same.
T (true) or F (false)?
1 Both speakers know someone who looks like them.
2 Most people have about two look-alikes in the world.
3 They recommend using the Internet to find a look-alike.

B ▶16 Listen again. Check (✓) the correct answers.
1 How did Luisa, the presenter, meet her look-alike?
   a ☐ At a party.
   b ☐ By chance.
   c ☐ They're relatives.
2 What do we know about her appearance?
   a ☐ She's tall.
   b ☐ She wears glasses.
   c ☐ She has brown eyes.
3 Why does Jacques believe we all have a look-alike?
   a ☐ Because he personally knows a lot of people with a look-alike.
   b ☐ Because there are very few facial shapes.
   c ☐ Because there are so many people in the world.
4 Why do they mention the Mongol emperor Genghis Khan?
   a ☐ He is the ancestor of many people alive today.
   b ☐ He had a twin brother who looked like him.
   c ☐ He had over 200 look-alikes.
5 What do they say about TwinStrangers.net?
   a ☐ It's free.
   b ☐ It uses illustrations.
   c ☐ It doesn't have many users.

Genghis Khan

C ▶16 Circle the correct option to complete the sentences. Listen again to check.
1 There was a woman next to me who was travelling *by / with* herself.
2 My husband said "You two look like *every / each* other."
3 That's natural, but we're talking about strangers who look like one *other / another*.
4 We like to have a very special image of *ourselves / us*.
5 You choose drawings that describe *you / yourself*.

D Complete 1–10 with one word in each gap.
1 My cousin and I look a lot like _____ other. People often think we're sisters!
2 Nobody wanted to go to Sicily with Jack, so he went by _____ .
3 I have five brothers and sisters. It's great. We all help one _____ around the house.
4 When I compared my photo with one of my granddad at the same age, I even surprised _____ . We look identical!
5 Actors like me are all the same. We don't like watching _____ when we're on TV or film.
6 Don't worry. Just be _____ at the interview.
7 Pete and Sara only talked to each _____ at the party.
8 That's the new head of marketing. Let's go over and introduce _____ .
9 I made some great friends at school. We've all kept in touch with one _____ since we left.
10 My aunt Rosie has lived by _____ since her husband passed away.

4.5 How many pairs of glasses do you own?

A Read the review quickly. How many stars is it (1–5)?

Adrift with the Oculus Rift ☆☆☆☆☆

a _____

The future of gaming has arrived with the Oculus Rift virtual reality headset. ¹For the m_ _t p_r_, when people think of virtual reality, they think of terrible graphics in 90s movies. You can forget that – with these goggles, you'll enter a new world of exploration.

b _____

Although the number of possible applications is endless, ²on av_ _ _g_, most people will use them for gaming. The games available are standard ones like soccer, and it is like you're in the stadium on the field.

c _____

When playing games, you use hand-held controllers. ³G_n_r_l_y speaking, they are easy to use, and you really feel like they are responding to your movements, especially in games where you explore space.

d _____

⁴By and l_ _g_, virtual reality headsets are incredibly heavy and cumbersome. It feels as if you are carrying a milk carton on your nose. Thankfully, the Oculus Rift is lightweight and comfortable.

e _____

In terms of sound quality, ⁵on the wh_ _ _, the headset is excellent. ⁶As a r_ _e, I like to use my own headphones with gadgets, and I was pleased that it was simple to hook these up to the device.

f _____

⁷Ov_r_ _l, the Oculus Rift is the ultimate gaming experience. The only danger is that you forget that there is another real world out there!

B Complete the paragraph headings (a–f) with 1–6.
1 Pleasant to wear
2 It feels as if you're really there
3 Remember there's a real world, too!
4 An exciting new device
5 Quickly reacts to hand actions
6 Compatible with other devices

C Complete the missing letters in the phrases for generalizing 1–7.

D Write your own conclusion to the product review in **A**. Do you think the Oculus Rift headset will catch on and become popular?

_____

_____

E Look back at lessons 4.1–4.5 in the Student's Book. Find the connection between the song lines and the content of each lesson.

F ▶17 Listen to the five question titles from the unit, and record your answers to them. If possible, compare recordings with a classmate.

5.1 What's your biggest life decision so far?

A ▶18 Match the sentence halves. There's one extra ending. Listen to the start of a podcast to check.

1. Golden Globe Award-winning actor Peter Dinklage has
2. However, like many actors, he had to overcome extreme
3. Moreover, as a "dwarf" (properly known as a "little person" today), Dinklage faced many
4. In fact, he had to say "no" to many early acting roles in order to pursue

a ☐ difficulties in finding decent parts to play.
b ☐ poverty at the beginning of his career.
c ☐ worked in a train station and as a waiter among other jobs.
d ☐ his dream of becoming a serious actor.
e ☐ achieved unbelievable success.

B ▶19 Listen to the whole podcast. Check (✓) the correct answers.

1. Dinklage's mom
   a ☐ had the same job as his dad.
   b ☐ worked in education.
   c ☐ was an actress.
2. Dinklage decided to become an actor
   a ☐ because he couldn't find any other work.
   b ☐ by chance.
   c ☐ when he was still a child.
3. In his early career, Dinklage refused to play
   a ☐ roles in commercial films.
   b ☐ fantasy characters.
   c ☐ comedy roles.
4. When he was a poor actor, his apartment
   a ☐ had animals living in it.
   b ☐ was incredibly hot.
   c ☐ was a long way away from the station.
5. According to the podcast, Dinklage's biggest decision was
   a ☐ accepting the role in *The Station Agent*.
   b ☐ leaving New Jersey.
   c ☐ refusing to play terrible roles.

C ▶19 Complete the sentences with a number. Listen again to check.

1. Dinklage was born in New Jersey in _____ .
2. He was in _____ grade when he heard his first big round of applause in a school play.
3. Dinklage says he often paid for his dinner in dimes – _____ cent pieces – because that was all he had.
4. In _____ , he starred in the movie *The Station Agent*.
5. His performance in *The Station Agent* was stunning, and won him a Golden Globe at the age of _____ .

D Cross out the incorrect option in each sentence.

1. It's not always easy in life to pursue your *ambition / goals / wish*.

2. We all face *destruction / obstacles / difficulties* in life. We have to confront them.

3. Work hard and you will achieve *a lot of money / good results / success*.

4. Learn to overcome your *fear of / luck at / problem with* the unknown.

5.2 What would you love to be able to do?

A ▶20 Complete the article with the correct form of the verbs. Listen to check.

Wishlist: What would you love to be able to do?

Kayleigh Bloom

That's easy – go surfing! If only my family ¹_____ (live) next to the ocean. People think everyone in Australia spends all day on the beach, but we live in Alice Springs, in the middle of the country. I couldn't live further from the coast.

How I wish my mom and dad ² _____ (have) a different job! My parents are farmers, and we have a farm with over 1,000 sheep, so we can't go anywhere else. Some days I wish they ³_____ (never / move) here. I wish I ⁴_____ (be) born in Sydney or somewhere like that.

If only I ⁵_____ (know) people with a house near the beach, then I could stay with them from time to time. I did have a friend who moved to Sydney and I wish I ⁶_____ (not / lost) contact with her. That would be perfect – Bondi Beach in the morning! Surf's up! If only …

B Correct the mistake in each sentence.

1 I wish I can swim. I can't believe I never learned. _____
2 My mom is always calling me on my cell phone. I wish she would do that! _____
3 I wish I didn't drop out of college. It was such a big mistake. _____
4 If only I have my credit card with me today, but I don't. _____
5 Rick always ignores me. If only he had replied to my emails from time to time. _____
6 I wish Martin hadn't put that terrible photo online, but he does, and now everyone has seen it. _____

C Circle the correct alternatives.

1 A: I'm never going to win the triathlon.
   B: Don't worry about winning. *Do / Make* the best you can.
2 A: This song is driving me crazy. I'm never going to learn how to play it.
   B: Keep *to / at* it! It takes time to learn these things.
3 A: I've applied for 50 jobs, and I haven't even had an interview.
   B: It's a bad time to look for work. Don't let it *get / getting* you down.
4 A: I think this course is a waste of time. I'm not learning anything new.
   B: Stick *in / with* it! You may be surprised what you learn by the end.
5 A: My presentation was a disaster. People were falling asleep listening to me!
   B: It happens to us all. *You / You'll* do better next time.

D Make it personal Write a true sentence about you to provoke these responses.

1 YOU: _____
   B: Do the best you can.
2 YOU: _____
   B: You'll do better next time.

How important is a college degree? 5.3

A Read and complete the article with these words. There are two extra words.

| international | overall | overestimate | overrated | overworked | underachievers |
| underestimate | underachievers | underpaid | underprivileged | underqualified |

"I don't want to go to school" "OK, then, don't!"

IT pioneers Bill Gates and Steve Jobs famously dropped out of college, but many never went to school at all. Instead, these kids were home-schooled, taught at home by their brave moms and dads, or by a specialist tutor.

There isn't much of an ¹_____ movement encouraging home-schooling worldwide because in many countries, it's simply illegal. However, it is common in the U.S., where there are around 1.8 million home-schooled children. Indeed, several experts warn we may ²_____ those numbers because many states don't require parents to register their children at all. There may well be a lot more.

Parents usually choose home-schooling because they feel their children are ³_____ , due to too much testing and homework in the current school system. Unfortunately, like it or not, tests equal results. Quite a few home-schooled children end their education ⁴_____ because they have no full high school diploma.

But it cuts both ways. Some students, on the other hand, who were ⁵_____ at school because of bullying, see a rapid improvement in their schoolwork when they start home-schooling. But what about the social side of things? Well, it's not necessarily a lonely life. People ⁶_____ the difficulty of making friends, but there are lots of sports teams and clubs where home-schooled children can meet other kids.

Whatever the benefits, however, at the end of the day, home-schooling will never be an option for children from ⁷_____ backgrounds. If their parents earn low salaries, and ⁸_____, they simply cannot afford to take time off from work to educate their children themselves. So, yet again, the rich get richer.

B Complete 1–6 with a form of the word in CAPITALS.

1 I feel that teachers are ___underpaid___. They deserve a much higher salary. PAID
2 Don't _____ this physics problem. Your essay must show how complicated it is. SIMPLIFY
3 The city college is really _____. Their courses are actually very good. RATED
4 My grandma is one of life's _____. She left school at 15, but she now runs a chain of 12 stores. ACHIEVERS
5 I failed my audition for drama school. They said I was _____. I was shouting and screaming, and my character didn't feel natural. ACTING
6 Our end-of-course project was a disaster. We _____ how much time we needed, and we almost didn't finish it. ESTIMATED

C Correct the mistake in each sentence.

1 James has hardly no work experience. _____
2 Reading academic journals isn't exactly interested. _____
3 My granddad has virtually none qualifications. _____
4 Studying for an online degree is nothing but easy. _____

5.4 Did you make any mistakes yesterday?

A Read the article below. Check (✓) the correct column.

	What Mr. Sabo intended to do	What Mr. Sabo actually did
1 wear his glasses		
2 buy a ticket from a cashier		
3 buy a ticket from a machine		
4 get one $30 ticket		
5 get two $20 tickets		

B Re-read. T (true) or F (false)?
1 Mr. Sabo doesn't mind waiting for things.
2 He frequently uses the machines in the store.
3 He spent less money than he intended.
4 He immediately realized that he was a winner.
5 Other people share in Mr. Sabo's success.
6 The store has recently closed down.

Oops ... I think I'm a winner

All eyeglass wearers have done it; put down our glasses and then completely forgotten where they were. Like Bob Sabo, but, ironically, if he'd found his glasses last week, he'd be a lot poorer now. Why? Easton, Connecticut resident Mr. Sabo left home without them, and won $30,000 as a result.

Mr. Sabo wouldn't have his hands on the $30,000 check if he hadn't gotten impatient in his local Super Shop & Stop store. There was a long line at the cash register so, for the first time, he used a machine in the store to buy his lottery ticket.

Mr. Sabo had wanted to buy his usual two $20 tickets, but accidentally pressed the button for one $30 ticket. If he'd pressed the right button, our story would end there, but Mr. Sabo had found the Midas touch. When he got home, he discovered that he was holding a winning ticket for $30,000! If he'd had his glasses on, his wallet would be a lot lighter today.

As a reward for selling the ticket, the store also gets $300 and all the publicity in the world. So, glasses or no glasses, it looks like those lines at the cash register aren't going to go away anytime soon.

C Complete the sentences with the correct form of the verbs.
1 If I _____ (not be) a native speaker of Portuguese, I wouldn't have gotten my job.
2 Just think! If you _____ (chose) 17 instead of 16, you would have won the lottery. You were so close to $500,000!
3 We _____ (live) in Japan today if our parents hadn't emigrated to Brazil back in 1999.
4 An old friend got in contact after 10 years. He _____ (not find) me online if I weren't on Facebook.
5 Aziz _____ (drive) you to the station tomorrow if he hadn't had that car accident last week.
6 My brother was so close to dropping out of college in 2011. Think about that. He _____ (not work) as a doctor now if he had.

D **Make it personal** Have you ever sent or received an email, photo, text, or Whatsapp® message by mistake? What happened? How did you feel?

_____
_____

How lucky are you? 5.5

Telling a story (2)

A Read the story and order the pictures 1–5.

Lightning doesn't strike the same place twice ... it can strike it seven times!

Everything was tranquil out on the lake on that day in June, 1977. Park ranger Roy Sullivan was quietly fishing when he noticed an odd smell in the air, like sulfur. It was a warning.

Suddenly, a lightning bolt struck him with devastating force, and he fell out of his boat. Shocked and exhausted, Roy swam to the shore, but his ordeal was not yet over. Badly burned and with black holes in his clothes, he crawled back to his car. If he thought he was safe, he was in for another surprise.

To Roy's horror, he discovered a huge black bear right next to his vehicle. The bear had come out of the woods and was eating the fish that Roy had caught. Most people would have been terrified, but the ranger just took a tree branch and hit the bear in the face, which frightened the animal away. Finally, Roy was able to drive to hospital, after the luckiest – or unluckiest – day of his life.

What's most amazing about this story is that it wasn't the first time that Roy Sullivan had been hit by lightning. In fact, it was the seventh lighting strike that the park ranger had survived, earning him a place in the *Guinness Book of Records*. He also claimed to have encountered bears over 20 times during his legendary career at Shenandoah National Park. They don't make park rangers like they used to.

B Find vivid adjectives in the text which are synonyms for 1–8.

1 peaceful and quiet (para 1) _____
2 powerful and destructive (para 2) _____
3 surprised and scared (para 2) _____
4 really tired (paragraph 2) _____
5 extremely large (para 3) _____
6 extremely scared (para 3) _____
7 surprising, incredible (para 4) _____
8 very, very famous (para 4) _____

C Complete a short entry about Roy for an online wiki. Use at least two bold vivid adjectives from B.

Legendary park ranger Roy Sullivan (1912–1983) _____
_____

D Look back at lessons 5.1–5.5 in the Student's Book. Find the connection between the song lines and the content of each lesson.

E ▶21 Listen to the five question titles from this unit, and record your answers to them. If possible, compare recordings with a classmate.

6 » 6.1 Have you ever Googled yourself?

A Cross out the option that doesn't work in each sentence.
1 We're worried about *journalists / hackers / teachers* entering the school website.
2 Someone broke into my *bag / car / website*, but I don't know if it's worth telling the police.
3 She was surprised when she looked *herself / the definition / the password* up online.
4 *Doctors / Flight attendants / Teachers* always keep records of the people they work with.

B ▶22 Listen to Isabella's tech tips and number these search engines in the order you hear them 1–4. What's the main topic of her broadcast?
1 what's wrong with Google® ☐
2 how Google became the world's top search engine ☐
3 Google's competitors ☐

C ▶22 Complete 1–4 with the search engines in **B**. Listen again to check, if necessary.
1 _____ is currently the most popular search engine.
2 _____ helps you maintain privacy when searching online.
3 _____ is pretty similar to Google.
4 _____ helps people find text and pictures that they don't have to pay for.

D ▶22 Listen again. Check (✓) the two conclusions you can draw from Isabella.
1 Most search engines have both advantages and disadvantages. ☐
2 People should stop using Google immediately. ☐
3 It's far too risky to use more than one search engine on their computer. ☐
4 Google is fine, but you might want to use others from time to time. ☐

E Add *is* four times to this quote.

> "The biggest risk not taking any risk ... In a world that changing really quickly, the only strategy that guaranteed to fail not taking risks."
>
> Mark Zuckerberg (Founder of Facebook)

Do you worry about your privacy? 6.2

A Rewrite what these people said using the passive form. Include the word in CAPITALS.

1 Someone took a video from my YouTube® account and used it without my permission. TAKEN
_____

2 Somebody hacked my blog, so when people looked at it, they saw an ad for second-hand cell phones. HAD
_____

3 It would shock you if you Googled yourself. BE
_____

4 My friends have put lots of photos of me on Facebook. BY
_____

5 A group of people are spreading a rumor about you on Twitter. BEING
_____

6 Nick asked a programmer to design his website for him. WAS
_____

B ▶23 Complete the conversation with these phrases. There's one extra. Listen to check.

| point taken | I don't see it that way | here's the thing | I admit |
| what's your take on it | couldn't agree more | believe it or not |

ADAM: Listen to this. A 22-year-old woman, Connor Riley, was offered a job by a major IT company. Immediately afterwards, she went on Twitter and complained she didn't like the trip to the office and hated the work. The company saw the tweet, and ¹_____ fired her before she started work!

KIRSTY: Whoa, Adam! That's not fair!

ADAM: Are you kidding? ²_____ . She insulted her new company. What kind of employee is that?

KIRSTY: ³_____ . Twitter is private! Why should her company be looking at her tweets?

ADAM: Twitter isn't private! That's why employees of big companies have to write things like "All opinions are my own" when they use it.

KIRSTY: OK, ⁴_____ , but I still think it's an invasion of privacy. Jason, ⁵_____ ?

JASON: Me? Well, I feel sorry for her. She makes one mistake at 22, and it's on the Internet forever.

ADAM: Absolutely! I ⁶_____ . That's why you have to be so careful about what you put online.

C Correct one mistake in each conversation.

1 A: I don't think people should use their smartphones when they're talking to you.
   B: I'm totally agree. It's really rude, isn't it? _____

2 A: I think we should ask for some help in designing our website. I don't think we can do it on our own.
   B: That does sense, I admit. _____

3 A: Listen to what I'm about saying. It's very important.
   B: OK. I'm all ears! _____

4 A: Why don't you want to be on Facebook?
   B: Look, here the thing. I don't want to tell everybody about everything I'm doing. I value my privacy.
   _____

5 A: If you try to write your essay in the middle of the night, you're going to make mistakes. Take your time with it.
   B: OK, OK! Point take. _____

D **Make it personal** Describe a time when someone you know wrote an inappropriate online post. What happened?

_____
_____

6.3 What makes you suspicious?

A Read the newspaper article. Check (✓) the correct question 1–3.

Digital Detective

Do you have a problem and no one else can help? Email it to … the Digital Detective!

1 Am I right to keep tabs on my son?
2 Are we being spied on through the computer?
3 Is the government eavesdropping on our online conversations?

Dear Digital Detective

My husband and I bought our 12-year old son his first computer, and he loves it. He's designing his own games, and he's set up a blog. We're so happy that he's enjoying writing ¹**it**, but there's just one problem. The computer's a laptop with a built-in camera, and our son's convinced he's being watched through it. He won't believe me when I say it's OK. Can you help me set his mind at rest?

Concerned mom

The Digital Detective replies …

It's natural to be afraid of being connected to almost everyone on the planet via the Internet. Personally, I'd be pleased that your son is conscious of these dangers. Many people his age are unaware of ²**them**.

Having said that, the camera is a threat. It's possible for other people to take control of this device. ³**They** break into your computer in the traditional way: using a virus on a website, so you need to ensure your antivirus is up-to-date. Also check that you have a password for your home WiFi, and make sure it's ⁴**one** that's hard to crack, because that's also a vulnerability.

You'll know if your webcam is active because a blue light appears when you're using it (look for ⁵**this** next time you make a call). If you don't see a light, it's unlikely anyone else is there.

If you're still concerned, there's one very basic way of avoiding unwanted surveillance. When you're not using the webcam, cover it up with a sock or a piece of paper. ⁶**That** will give them a black screen to stare at!

B What do the bold words in the article refer to?
1 _his blog_
2 _____
3 _____
4 _____
5 _____
6 _____

C Check (✓) the sentences that you can infer from the article.

The Digital Detective …
1 has some sympathy for the son. ☐
2 doesn't think teenagers appreciate the risks presented by the Internet. ☐
3 believes that there is a solution to every online threat. ☐
4 thinks that almost every home computer is infected with a virus. ☐
5 enjoys low-tech solutions to high-tech problems. ☐

D Read the graffiti, then complete the sentence so that it expresses your opinion.

Suspicion is the cancer of friendship.
Suspicion and doubt lead to animosity and hatred.
Secrets don't destroy things, but suspicion does.
Suspicion often creates what it suspects.

For me, suspicion _____.

Are you into social media? 6.4

A Read the article below and check (✓) the best summary.
1 A supermarket worker posted a question on the Internet and made thousands of new friends. ☐
2 An ordinary guy became famous because a customer where he worked thought he was attractive and tweeted his photo. ☐

B ▶ 24 Re-read and circle the correct alternatives. Listen to check.

Alex from Target becomes the Target!

"There's one thing in life worse than being talked about, and that's not being talked about." ¹*Whenever / Whichever* the Irish author Oscar Wilde said that, it clearly wasn't during the Internet age. It's one thing for a celebrity to face media exposure, but ²*whichever / whoever* thought that the full glare of public interest could fall on an everyday supermarket employee?

Alex Lee was working at his local Target supermarket when a teenage girl, struck by his good looks, snapped his photo. ³*However / Whatever* it happened, the image turned up on Tumblr®, and then Twitter with the hashtag #Alexfromtarget. It created a Twitter frenzy with 800,000 retweets over the course of the day. ⁴*Whichever / Whoever* site you looked at, Alex was trending.

⁵*However / Whatever* else Alex was doing that day, he wasn't expecting to become world famous. It was only at the end of his shift that he checked his cell phone and discovered he had thousands of new followers. His innocent next tweet then went viral:

Alex Lee ✓   ≗+ Follow
@AlexLeeWorld

Am i famous now?

RETWEETS   LIKES
37,536   82,501

3:09 p.m. - 2 Nov 2014

the bemused worker wondered.

The answer is yes — and he's now seeking a career as a musician with his own site on YouTube.

C Match 1–5 to a–f to make sentences. There is one extra ending.
1 I get my smartphone out and check Facebook
2 I never agree to be online friends with someone I haven't met
3 I'm pretty patient. I'll wait to connect to the WiFi
4 Photo quality is never great online
5 I never reply to Twitter abuse

a ☐ whichever site you use to upload them.
b ☐ whenever I'm on public transportation.
c ☐ whatever they say about me.
d ☐ however long it takes.
e ☐ whatever you like.
f ☐ whoever they are.

D **Make it personal** Complete the sentences so they're true for you.
1 I go online whenever _____.
2 I use my smartphone to watch whatever _____.
3 Wherever I go, I keep my cell phone on, except _____.

6.5 Who do you share your secrets with?

A how to ... guide

How to keep your smartphone safe

Almost everyone has an anti-virus program on their computer, but large numbers of people have no security protection on their smartphone. So how can you keep your smartphone safe? Here are six top tips.

A _____
As
¹S̶o̶ far as possible, use the latest updates for your phone. Even if you don't have an anti-virus, this will ensure that the major security holes stay closed.

B _____
²Never not ever click on a link in a text message or email from an unknown source. This is one of the most common ways of inserting malware – dangerous programs – onto your handheld device.

C _____
Get a "find my phone" app. This will tell you where your phone is if it gets lost. ³However you do, do not approach someone who has stolen your phone. This can be a dangerous situation.

D _____
Lock your screen with a password. ⁴Avoid to use programs that don't have a password with letters, numbers, and symbols.

E _____
If you use your phone for online shopping, ⁵be sure use a site with a "https" in the address bar, like https://www.amazon.com. The final -s indicates that it is secure.

F _____
⁶Make your best to use private, not public, WiFi networks. Unwanted listeners may be eavesdropping on your conversations.

A Read the article and check (✓) what you think is the most important tip (A–F).

B Re-read and correct the mistakes in the underlined phrases 1–6.

C Match the headings 1–7 to paragraphs A–F. There's one extra.
1 Make it difficult to log on to your device.
2 Never use your real name.
3 Don't respond to strangers when they contact you.
4 Avoid going online in cafés and public places.
5 Keep your smartphone up-to-date.
6 Look carefully at the URL before you buy.
7 Find your phone with an app.

D Add one more guideline to explain how to keep your smartphone safe.
_____
_____
_____

E Look back at lessons 6.1–6.5 in the Student's Book. Find the connection between the song lines and the content of each lesson.

F ▶25 Listen to the five question titles from the unit, and record your answers to them. If possible, compare recordings with a classmate.

Selected audio scripts

3 page 6 exercises A and B

J = Jackie, K = Ki-Yeon

J: What are those, Ki-Yeon?
K: What?
J: These wooden birds.
K: Oh, they're wooden ducks. In Korea, it's traditional to give wooden ducks like these as a wedding gift. They're a present from my future mother-in-law, Soo.
J: They're really cute.
K: Yeah. Soo's such a lovely lady. She'll be the perfect mother-in-law.
J: So, how are the preparations going? It's hard to organize a wedding, isn't it?
K: Hard? It's a nightmare. Do you have any difficult people in your family?
J: I only have difficult people in my family! What's the problem?
K: We want to have a traditional Korean wedding, OK? So usually the parents pay for the wedding. Each family pays half the money.
J: So?
K: David, my stepfather, doesn't want to pay. He thinks it's too expensive. It's no use discussing it with him. He refuses to pay his half.
J: Oh no!
K: And that's not all. I asked my brother, Pete, well, my half-brother, to prepare the wedding invitations.
J: Uh-huh.
K: He hasn't done it yet. Pete hasn't sent any wedding invitations to anyone. He's always like this. It's impossible for him to do anything quickly!
J: When is the wedding?
K: In July.
J: And it's now February.
K: Right. We don't have a lot of time.
J: Any other problems?
K: The food! My cousin runs a restaurant and she agreed to provide the catering.
J: Well, that's one problem solved.
K: No, it's not. She's now expecting a baby on the day of the wedding!
J: Maybe a new caterer would be better. Is anyone else in your family helping you?
K: Hmm ... My aunt, Min-Jun. She wants to help, so she calls me all the time. Yesterday, she asked me about the flowers for the ceremony, and the phone call took an hour! An hour!
J: OK, OK. Keep calm. Look, Ki-Yeon, you can't arrange this wedding on your own. It's essential for you to get some help. Talk to your friends. Ask them to help you because you have an awful lot of things to do over the next few months!
K: Tell me about it!

6 page 11 exercises A and B

F = Frank Mortimer, R = Rachel Schultz, A = Dr Alba Lopez

F: It all began in March 1995 in Puerto Rico. A farmer discovered eight sheep in a field with all their blood missing. This was the first recorded case of the chupacabra, the goat-sucker, a mysterious monster that drinks the blood of animals. Welcome to *Science Fiction or Science Fact*? I'm Frank Mortimer. I'm here with author and journalist, Rachel Schultz. She investigates animals that may or may not exist. Rachel, hello.
R: Hi Frank.
F: So, tell us, what does the chupacabra look like?
R: Well, eyewitnesses say that the chupacabra is a big gray animal with red eyes. It moves like a kangaroo and it has spines on its back.
F: You can't be serious!
R: Many different witnesses have seen the animal. They all give the same description. I'm pretty sure they're telling the truth.
F: I doubt that, but OK. And, where have people seen the chupacabra?
R: Since the first sighting in 1995, there have been reports of chupacabras in Puerto Rico, the continental United States, Mexico, and Chile.
F: Chile too? So, not just North America. Hmm. Does it attack people?
R: No, all the records show attacks on animals such as goats, ...
F: Obviously.
R: Dogs, and cows.
F: Rachel, thank you. Now, I think we have Dr Alba Lopez on the line, a biologist from Puerto Rico. Alba?
A: Hello? Hello?
F: Alba, hi, it's Frank here on *Science Fiction or Science Fact*? Can you hear me?
A: Yes, I can.
F: Dr Alba Lopez, you're a biologist. The chupacabra doesn't really exist, does it? I mean, anything might have killed those animals.
A: I really doubt that there's a blood-sucking monster with red eyes out there!
F: So, how do you explain the stories of the chupacabra?
A: Well, something must have killed these animals, that's for sure. I think it might have been a coyote.
F: A coyote? A wild dog? How do you explain that?
A: The coyote might have been ill. When they're ill, coyotes can become thin and gray, like descriptions of the chupacabra. And coyotes kill and eat farm animals all the time.
F: Rachel, your thoughts?
R: It can't have been a coyote. These farmers know about animals. It might have been an animal unknown to science.
F: Well, there we have it. A new, mystery animal or a sick coyote. Rachel, Alba, thank you both. So, what do you think? If you want to get in on the debate, log onto our website and leave a comment. We look forward to hearing your thoughts.

11 page 16 exercises A and B

Conversation 1

I = Interviewer, R = Ron

I: What was your favorite activity as a child, Ron?
R: Er ... let me think. Um, well, when I was about 13, I loved role-playing games.
I: Role-playing games? Like Dungeons and Dragons?
R: Yeah, you know, you imagine you're a hero or a wizard and you have all kinds of adventures with your friends. You get these big rule books and you also need dice to play. It was pretty complicated.
I: Did you use to dress up? Wear special costumes or masks?
R: No! We didn't use to wear any special clothes. It was all about using your imagination. We used to play on the dining table at home. We'd always get some nachos and sodas and we would play for hours.
I: Did lots of people use to do this?
R: Absolutely! It was a huge fad back in the 1980s. Remember, we didn't have cell phones, X boxes or the internet, so we had to create our own fantasies much more.
I: Of course! Different times. And, do you still play these games?
R: Hmm, well I used to play them in college but I stopped many years ago. I have a son and a daughter now and when they're a bit older I might introduce them to the games. Why not? They're a lot of fun. If I can get them away from their phones, of course.

Conversation 2

I = Interviewer, M = Mary

I: What was your favorite activity as a child, Mary?
M: When I was 12, roller-blading was a huge fad. I used to love it!
I: I had a pair of skates once too! Loved them. Where did you use to go roller-blading?
M: My dad would take me to the park. Sometimes I'd go rollerblading with my friends too. Everyone had rollerblades back then. We used to love them.
I: How did you get into it?
M: Well, my best friend had a pair of rollerblades and I thought they were so cool. I used to talk about them all the time and so my parents bought me a pair for my twelfth

63

Selected audio scripts

birthday. They were black and so was my helmet. I still have them today actually, stored away somewhere. Even though they don't fit any more, I just can't seem to throw them away.

I: Really? Do you still go roller-blading these days?

M: Sadly not. I had an accident once when I was about 14. Horrible! I was skating along a bike path, hit a stone, fell and broke my leg! I couldn't walk for a whole summer. It was just awful, scary too, and it turned me off roller-blading after that.

16 page 21 exercises A, B and C

L = Luisa, J = Jacques

L: I was on a flight the other day from New York to L.A. and there was a woman next to me who was traveling by herself. She looked familiar and then my husband said, you two look like each other. And it was true. We both had long straight hair and brown eyes. We took a selfie to prove it. It was weird. That's what has inspired my big question today. Do we all have a double? Jacques?

J: It's very likely, Luisa. There isn't an infinite number of genes. In a population of millions, it's very possible that someone will look like you. I myself look a lot like a good friend. People often think we're brothers.

L: Uh-huh. People often look like family members. That's natural but we're talking about strangers who look like one another.

J: What is a stranger? Many people share a common ancestor. For example, 1 in every 200 men alive today is a descendant of Genghis Khan. Genghis Khan was the emperor of Mongolia and he died in 1227. So if you do the math, he by himself is a direct ancestor of an enormous number of people alive today.

L: Is it possible that we have *more* than one double?

J: We like to have a very special image of ourselves. We're all individuals. In fact, some experts believe we may each have seven lookalikes in the world.

L: How can people prove it?

J: I don't know about "prove it" but there are websites out there. One is TwinStrangers.net.

L: How does it work?

J: You choose drawings that describe yourself. You then compare the details with the information from other users on the site. If someone has a similar description, you look at the photos and see if you have found your lookalike.

L: Is it free?

J: No, you pay to use the site, but there is a Facebook group too.

L: Amazing, I might try it myself.

18 & 19 page 23 exercises A, B and C

Golden Globe Award-winning actor Peter Dinklage has achieved unbelievable success. However, like many actors, he had to overcome extreme poverty at the beginning of his career. Moreover, as a "dwarf" (properly known as a "little person" today), Dinklage faced many difficulties in finding decent parts to play. In fact, he had to say "no" to many early roles in order to pursue his dream of becoming a serious actor.

Dinklage was born in New Jersey in 1969. He wasn't from an acting family at all. His dad was a salesperson and his mom was a teacher, but Dinklage loved theater from an early age. He was in 5th grade when he heard his first big round of applause in a school play.

Eager to start an acting career, Dinklage moved to New York City in 1991 and it was there that his problems began.

Dinklage has dwarfism, which means his adult height is around 1.27 meters. There are plenty of roles for actors of that size, but Dinklage refused to take them. He didn't want to play magical creatures like elves in ads and children's movies. He preferred to wait for appropriate roles, which meant he often starved. He lived in a small apartment, where he could hear the trains going by. The apartment also had rats. Dinklage says he sometimes paid for his dinner in dimes – 10 cent pieces – because he had no other money.

Fortunately, his career slowly took off. In 2003, he starred in the movie *The Station Agent* which was an independent hit. Finally people were noticing Dinklage for his talent.

Then everything changed when he became one of the stars of the fantasy series *Game of Thrones* in 2011. His performance was incredible, and it won him a Golden Globe at the age of 42. Finally Dinklage had triumphed. And the biggest decision of his life had been saying "no" to all those terrible roles in the past.

22 page 28 exercises B, C and D

P = Presenter, I = Isabelle Sharpe

P: And now over to Isabella Sharpe, our new "tech tips" specialist.

I: Hello. What's the first website you look at in the morning? What's your home page? What's your first stop to finding out anything? For most people, the answer is probably Google. But, is Google the only search engine in town? Certainly not. It's just one of a range of possible websites you can use. So, what alternatives are there? Let's look at three of them.

Perhaps the competitor to Google that most people have heard of is Microsoft's Bing. To look up information, it works in a very similar way to Google. Some people suggest that Google is still slightly better than Bing at some searches, but they aren't so different.

DuckDuckGo is an indie. It's a search engine from a small start-up, and much less well-known. It's just as good but, unlike Google, DuckDuckGo does not track your movements online. The fact that it records user data is a serious drawback of using Google. If you are searching for something and you want to keep it a secret, like a new job when you're in the office, DuckDuckGo is a risk-free alternative.

Finally, there's CCSearch. Now they say that they are not a search engine but the program works very much like one. CCSearch helps you find images and content that you can use for free. Perhaps you are self-publishing a book and you need some photos, but you don't have any money. CCSearch will find free photos for you to use. However, you may still have to pay third parties for these images. Be aware that you use the site at your own risk.

Whichever way you look at it, Google has set the standard for search engines and continues to lead the pack. It's easy-to-use interface, along with its rapid, efficient search results, meant it really does deserve its place at the summit. Having said that, nothing lasts forever, and the younger competitors are starting to want a piece of the action.

That's all for now. I'm Isabella Sharpe. Thank you so much for listening.

Answer key

Unit 1

1.1
A 1 mother-in-law 2 step daughter
    3 great grandfather/granddad
    4 only child 5 twins 6 brother/cousin
B 1 single 2 stepfather/stepdad
    3 half-brother 4 only 5 father-in-law
C 1 made up 2 runs in 3 get along
    4 look up 5 look after
D Students' own answers

1.2
A Students' own answers
B 1 become 2 understand 3 have an opportunity 4 arrive at 5 received 6 becomes
C 1 Not asking for help is a bad idea.
    2 It started raining, but we carried on playing tennis.
    3 It's not worth going to the exhibit on Sunday.
    4 Having a new baby is totally exhausting.
    5 I can't help feeling nervous about next week's exams.
    6 I have a hard time thinking of new ideas for work.
D Students' own answers

1.3
A 2
B 1 b 2 e 3 a
C 1 ownership 2 affectionate
    3 neighborhood 4 helpful 5 freedom
    6 talkative 7 careless 8 happiness
D Students' own answers

1.4
A 1 family doesn't want to pay for the wedding
    2 brother hasn't taken care of the invitations yet
    3 cousin can't come to the wedding
    4 aunt is calling him a lot
B 1 T 2 F 3 F 4 F 5 T 6 F
C 1 It's essential for you to tell
    2 It's better not to give
    3 It's advisable to send
    4 It's hard not to get
    5 It's a good idea for you to ask
    6 There's no point choosing
D Students' own answers

1.5
A 1 it's important 2 To begin with
    3 On top of that 4 Besides 5 Lastly
B 1 c 2 b 3 a
C Students' own answers
D 1 family words 2 being young 3 pets, like a dog 4 the grammar: hard to (adjective + infinitive) 5 making voice calls
E Students' own answers

Unit 2

2.1
A Across: 1 clock 4 issues 5 crash
    6 brain 7 patterns
    Down: 2 leisure 3 dinner 4 instant
    7 peer
B 1 romantic relationships 2 Financial problems 3 material possessions
    4 Physical appearance 5 scientific fact
C 1 worry worrying 2 think to about
    3 making to make 4 to think thinking
    5 consider 'm considering
D Students' own answers

2.2
A 1 wears off 2 weight gain 3 treat
    4 at a disadvantage 5 a big deal
    6 keep you going
B 1 with 2 thing 3 of 4 eating 5 is
C 1 that 2 worst 3 it can place 4 that
    5 These are 6 of 7 are 8 being
    9 keeping 10 with

2.3
A The author believes it's more important to look intelligent.
B 1 of 2 at 3 to 4 at 5 at 6 for
C 3 and 5
D 1 second 2 its 3 which 4 them
    5 one 6 whose

2.4
A Doesn't believe it exists: Frank Mortimer, Alba Lopez
    Thinks it might exist: Rachel Schultz
B 1 goats sheep 2 brown red
    3 Argentina Mexico 4 tired thin
C 1 must 2 might just want 3 have been
    4 may exist
D 1 have seen 2 have been 3 have left
    4 have made 5 have rained

2.5
A 1 while 2 One advantage of 3 A further advantage 4 a number of drawbacks
    5 On the one hand 6 On the other hand
    7 To sum up
B 1 F 2 F 3 A 4 A
C Students' own answers
D 1 thinking about things, what's on your mind 2 food, eating out 3 ways to learn and be intelligent 4 spaceships, UFOs and science fiction 5 being a genius, having a high IQ
E Students' own answers

Unit 3

3.1
A 1 yawn 2 push 3 trip 4 stare 5 pull
    6 glance 7 scream 8 picture a
B 1 pushed 2 yawned 3 glanced
    4 screamed 5 whispered
C 1 go 2 happens 3 know 4 then
    5 believe 6 thing

3.2
A 1 was traveling 2 took 3 was working
    4 captured 5 had been waiting
    6 appeared 7 arrived 8 hit 9 had put
    10 went
B 1 was walking 2 dropped 3 had been taking / had taken 4 were camping
    5 had left 6 was watching
C Students' own answers

3.3
A The author likes it: the toasting knife
    The author doesn't like it: PEG
    The author gives no opinion: ice cream
B 1 slice 2 vegans 3 it's up to me
    4 pricey 5 stick 6 handy 7 pops up
    8 glow-in-the-dark
C 1 downs 2 cons 3 soul 4 worse
    5 face 6 over

3.4
A 1 Mary 2 Ron 3 Ron 4 Mary
    5 Mary 6 Ron
B 1 F 2 T 3 F 4 T 5 F 6 F
C 1 my mom bought me a surfboard
    2 We won the State Championship
    3 I used to collect / I would collect
    4 I didn't use to have any hobbies
D Students' own answers

3.5
A 1 as 2 Initially 3 Some time later
    4 in the meantime 5 Eventually
    6 All of a sudden 7 Finally
B 1 Initially 2 while 3 In the meantime
    4 Finally 5 suddenly 6 After a while
C 1 suddenly sudden 2 late later
    3 meanwhile meantime 4 it initially
    5 after a while
D 1 ways of looking: stare, glance 2 selfies
    3 binomials: safe and sound
    4 the grammar: used to
    5 happiness and feeling happy
E Students' own answers

Unit 4

4.1
A 1 out 2 in 3 out 4 for 5 out
    6 away 7 apart
B 1 Surely you'll agree that
    2 doesn't mean it's authentic
    3 Look at it this way.
    4 You're missing the point!
    5 Let me put it another way.
C Students' own answers

4.2
A 1 F 2 F 3 T
B 1 Even though 2 Unlike 3 whereas
    4 In spite 5 Despite
C 1 c 2 f 3 a 4 e 5 b
D Students' own answers

67

Answer key

4.3

A 1 d 2 f 3 a 4 c 5 e
B 1 In the end 2 At first 3 Back in the day 4 at some point 5 From time to time 6 in no time
C 1 wildfire 2 cats and dogs 3 the wind 4 a broken record 5 a glove 6 a bird

4.4

A 1 T 2 F 3 T
B 1 b 2 c 3 c 4 a 5 b
C 1 by 2 each 3 another 4 ourselves 5 yourself
D 1 each 2 himself 3 another 4 myself 5 ourselves 6 yourself 7 other 8 ourselves 9 another 10 herself

4.5

A 5 stars
B a 4 b 2 c 5 d 1 e 6 f 3
C 1 for the most part 2 average 3 Generally speaking 4 By and large 5 on the whole 6 As a rule 7 Overall
D Students' own answers
E 1 being deceived by appearances 2 the potential end of schooling 3 hearing gossip spread by others "through the grapevine" 4 the grammar: *each other* 5 the expression *dying for* (in the song line is used literally, not figuratively)
F Students' own answers

Unit 5

5.1

A a 3 b 2 d 4 e 1
B 1 b 2 c 3 b 4 a 5 c
C 1 1969 2 5th 3 10 4 2003 5 42
D 1 wish 2 destruction 3 a lot of money 4 luck at

5.2

A 1 lived 2 had 3 had never moved 4 had been 5 knew 6 hadn't lost
B 1 ~~can~~ could 2 ~~would~~ wouldn't 3 ~~didn't drop~~ hadn't dropped 4 ~~have~~ had 5 ~~had replied~~ replied 6 ~~does~~ did
C 1 Do 2 at 3 get 4 with 5 You'll
D Students' own answers

5.3

A 1 international 2 underestimate 3 overworked 4 underqualified 5 underachievers 6 overestimate 7 underprivileged 8 underpaid
B 1 underpaid 2 oversimplify 3 underrated 4 overachievers 5 overacting 6 underestimated
C 1 hardly ~~no~~ any 2 ~~interested~~ interesting 3 ~~none~~ no 4 ~~nothing~~ anything

5.4

A Intended: 1, 2, 5   Did: 3, 4
B 1 F 2 F 3 T 4 F 5 T 6 F
C 1 hadn't been 2 had chosen 3 would live / would be living 4 wouldn't have found 5 would have driven / would drive 6 wouldn't be working
D Students' own answers

5.5

A 1 b 2 d 3 a 4 c 5 e
B 1 tranquil 2 devastating 3 shocked 4 exhausted 5 huge 6 terrified 7 amazing 8 legendary
C Students' own answers
D 1 being someone's hero 2 the grammar: wishing, an imaginary situation 3 dropping out of college and not getting a degree 4 regretting a mistake, wishing to go back to yesterday and retract it 5 not being very lucky (because he wasn't born into a powerful family)
E Students' own answers

Unit 6

6.1

A 1 teachers 2 bag 3 the password 4 Flight attendants
B Topic 3 1 Google 2 Bing 3 DuckDuckGo 4 CCSearch
C 1 Google 2 DuckDuckGo 3 Bing 4 CCSearch
D 1 and 4
E risk is not, that is changing, that is guaranteed, is not taking

6.2

A 1 A video from my YouTube account has been taken and used without my permission.
2 I had my blog hacked so when people looked at it, they saw an ad for second-hand cell phones.
3 You would be shocked if you Googled yourself.
4 Lots of photos of me have been put on Facebook by my friends.
5 A rumor about you is being spread on Twitter (by a group of people).
6 A programmer was asked by Nick to design his website for him.
B 1 believe it or not. 2 Here's the thing. 3 I don't see it that way. 4 point taken 5 what's your take on it 6 couldn't agree more
C 1 I totally agree. 2 That makes sense. 3 Listen to what I'm about to say. 4 Look, here's the thing. 5 Point taken.
D Students' own answers

6.3

A 2
B 1 his blog 2 these dangers 3 people (who take control of the camera) 4 a password 5 a blue light 6 covering the webcam
C 1, 2 and 5
D Students' own answers

6.4

A 2
B 1 Whenever 2 whoever 3 However 4 Whichever 5 Whatever
C 1 b 2 f 3 d 4 a 5 c
D Students' own answers

6.5

A Students' own answers
B 1 As far as possible 2 Never ever 3 Whatever you do 4 Avoid using 5 be sure to use 6 Do your best
C A 5 B 3 C 7 D 1 E 6 F 4
D Students' own answers
E 1 offering somebody protection 2 privacy, not being able to contact someone 3 being spied upon 4 the grammar: question words with -ever 5 keeping (or not keeping) secrets
F Students' own answers

Phrasal verb list

Phrasal verbs are verbs with two or three words: main verb + particle (either a preposition or an adverb). The definitions given below are some of those introduced in iDentities. For a full list, visit www.richmondidentites.com

Transitive phrasal verbs have a direct object; some are separable, others inseparable

Phrasal verb	Meaning
A	
ask someone **over**	invite someone
B	
block something **out**	prevent from passing through
blow something **out**	extinguish (a candle)
bring something **about**	cause to happen
bring something **out**	introduce a new product
bring someone **up**	raise (a child)
bring something **up**	bring to someone's attention
C	
call someone **in**	ask for someone's presence
call something **off**	cancel
carry something **out**	conduct an experiment / plan
cash in on something	profit
catch up on something	get recent information
charge something **up**	charge with electricity
check someone / something **out**	examine closely
check up on someone	make sure a person is OK
cheer someone **up**	make happier
clear something **up**	clarify
come away with something	learn something useful
come down to something	be the most important point
come down with something	get an illness
come up with something	invent
count on someone / something	depend on
cut someone **off**	interrupt someone
cut something **off**	remove; stop the supply of
cut something **out**	remove; stop doing an action
D	
do something **over**	do again
draw something **together**	unite
dream something **up**	invent
drop someone / something **off**	take someplace
drop out of something	quit
E	
end up with something	have an unexpected result
F	
face up to something	accept something unpleasant
fall back on something	use an old idea
fall for someone	feel romantic love
fall for something	be tricked into believing
figure someone / something **out**	understand with thought
fill someone **in**	explain
find something **out**	learn information
follow something **through**	complete
G	
get something **across**	help someone understand
get around to something	finally do something
get away with something	avoid the consequences
get off something	leave (a bus, train, plane)
get on something	board (a bus, train, plane)
get out of something	leave (a car); avoid doing something
get to someone	upset someone
get to something	reach
get together with someone	meet

Phrasal verb	Meaning
give something **back**	return quit
give something **up**	stop hoping for change / trying to make something happen
give up on someone / something	agree
go along with something	stop doing (over time, as one becomes an adult)
grow out of something	
H	
hand something **in**	submit
hand something **out**	distribute
help someone **out**	assist
K	
keep someone or something **away**	cause to stay at a distance
keep something **on**	not remove (clothing / jewelry)
keep someone or something **out**	prevent from entering
keep up with someone	stay in touch
L	
lay someone **off**	fire for economic reasons
lay something **out**	arrange
leave something **on**	not turn off (a light or appliance); not remove (clothing or jewelry)
leave something **out**	not include, omit
let someone **down**	disappoint
let someone **off**	allow to leave (a bus, train); not punish
light something **up**	illuminate
look after someone / something	take care of
look down on someone	think one is better, disparage
look into something	research
look out for someone	watch, protect
look someone / something **up**	try to find
look up to someone	admire, respect
M	
make something **up**	invent
make up for something	do something to apologize
miss out on something	lose the chance
P	
pass something **out**	distribute
pass someone / something **up**	reject, not use
pay someone **back**	repay, return money
pay someone **off**	bribe
pay something **off**	pay a debt
pick someone **up**	give someone a ride
pick something **up**	get / buy; learn something; answer the phone; get a disease
point someone / something **out**	indicate, show
put something **away**	return to its appropriate place
put something **back**	return to its original place
put someone **down**	treat with disrespect
put something **off**	delay
put something **together**	assemble, build
put something **up**	build, erect
put up with someone / something	accept without complaining
R	
run into someone	meet
run out of something	not have enough

119

Phrasal verb list

Phrasal verb	Meaning
S	
see something **through**	complete
send something **back**	return
send something **out**	mail
set something **up**	establish; prepare for use
settle on something	choose after consideration
show someone / something **off**	display the best qualities
shut something **off**	stop (a machine, light, supply)
sign someone **up**	register
stand up for someone / something	support
stick with / to someone / something	not quit, persevere
straighten something **up**	make neat
switch something **on**	start, turn on (a machine, light)
T	
take something **away**	remove
take something **back**	return; accept an item; retract a statement
take something **in**	notice, remember; make a clothing item smaller
take someone **on**	hire
take something **on**	agree to a task
take someone **out**	invite and pay for someone
take something **up**	start a new activity (as a habit)
talk someone **into**	persuade
talk something **over**	discuss
tear something **down**	destroy, demolish
tear something **up**	tear into small pieces
think back on something	remember
think something **over**	consider
think something **up**	invent, think of a new idea
touch something **up**	improve with small changes
try something **on**	put on to see if it fits, is desirable (clothing, shoes)
try something **out**	use an item / do an activity to see if it's desirable
turn something **around**	turn so the front faces the back; cause to get better
turn someone / something **down**	reject
turn something **in**	submit
turn someone / something **into**	change from one type or form to another
turn someone **off**	cause to lose interest, feel negatively
turn something **out**	make, manufacture
U	
use something **up**	use completely, consume
W	
wake someone **up**	cause to stop sleeping
walk out on someone	leave a spouse / child / romantic relationship
watch out for someone	protect
wipe something **out**	remove, destroy
work something **out**	calculate mathematically; solve a problem
write something **down**	create a written record (on paper)
write something **up**	write in a finished form

Intransitive phrasal verbs
have no direct object; they are all inseparable

Phrasal verb	Meaning
A	
act up	behave inappropriately
B	
break down	stop functioning
break out	start suddenly (a war, fire, disease)
C	
catch on	become popular
check in	report arrival (at a hotel, airport)
check out	pay a bill and leave (a hotel)
cheer up	become happier
come along	go with, accompany
come back	return
come up	arise (an issue)
D	
dress up	wear more formal clothes; a costume
drop in	visit unexpectedly
drop out	quit
E	
eat out	eat in a restaurant
F	
find out	learn new information
follow through	finish, complete something
G	
get ahead	make progress, succeed
get along	have a good relationship
get by	survive
get through	finish; survive
go along	accompany; agree
go away	leave a place
go on	continue
H	
hang up	end a phone call
hold on	wait (often during a phone call)
K	
keep away	stay at a distance
keep on	continue
keep out	not enter
L	
light up	illuminate; look pleased, happy
look out	be careful
M	
make up	end an argument
miss out	lose the chance (for something good)
P	
pass out	become unconscious, faint
pay off	be worthwhile
pick up	improve
R	
run out	leave suddenly; not have enough
S	
show up	appear
sign up	register
slip up	make a mistake
stay up	not go to bed
T	
take off	leave, depart (a plane)
turn in	go to sleep
turn out	have a certain result
turn up	appear
W	
watch out	be careful